THE CHRISTIAN'S GREAT INTEREST

William Guthrie

THE BANNER OF TRUTH TRUST

THE BANNER OF TRUTH TRUST
3 Murrayfield Road, Edinburgh EH12 6EL
PO Box 621, Carlisle, Pennsylvania 17013, USA

*

First published 1658
First Banner of Truth Trust edition, 1969
Reprinted 1982
Reprinted 1994
Reprinted 1997
Reprinted 2002
ISBN 0 85151 354 9

*

Printed in Finland by
WS Bookwell

To the Reader

CHRISTIAN READER:

While the generality of men, especially in these days, by their eager pursuit after low and base interests, have proclaimed, as upon the house tops, how much they have forgotten to make choice of that better part, which, if chosen, should never be taken from them; I have made an essay, such as it is, in the following Treatise, to take thee off from this unprofitable, though painful pursuit, by proposing the chiefest of interests, even the Christian's Great Interest, to be seriously pondered and constantly pursued by thee. Thou mayst think it strange to see anything in print from my pen, as it is indeed a surprise to myself; but necessity hath made me, for this once, to offer so much violence to my own inclination, in regard that some, without my knowledge, have lately published some imperfect notes of a few of my sermons, most confusedly cast together, prefixing withal this vain title, as displeasing to myself as the publishing of the thing, 'A Clear Attractive Warming Beam,' &c. Upon this occasion was I prevailed with to publish this late piece, wherein I have purposely used a homely and plain style, lest otherwise – though, when I have stretched myself to the utmost, I am below the judicious and more understanding – I should be above the reach of the rude and ignorant, whose advantage I have mainly, if not only, consulted. I have, likewise, studied brevity in everything, so far as I conceived it to be consistent with plainness and perspicuity; knowing that the persons to whom I address myself herein, have neither much money to spend upon books, nor much time to spare in reading. If thou be a rigid critic, I know thou mayst meet with several things to carp at; yet assure thyself, that I had no design to offend thee, neither will thy simple approbation satisfy me. It is thy edification I intend, together with the incitements of some others, more expert and experienced in this excellent subject, to handle the same to greater length, which I have more briefly hinted at, who am thy servant in the work of the gospel,

William Guthrie

CONTENTS

Part II How to attain a saving interest in Christ

Memoir of the Author

William Guthrie, one of the holiest and ablest of the experimental divines of Scotland, was born at Pitforthy, the seat of his ancestors, in the shire of Angus, in the year 1620. The branch of the house of Guthrie from which he sprang was ancient and honourable; and its interest in the cause of truth and godliness was proved by the fact, that four of the children had early been devoted to the ministry of the gospel. The only one of these who did not obtain a fixed charge was Robert, who soon lost health and life by his abundant labours in the cause of Christ; Alexander was settled at Stracathro, within his native shire, in 1645, and continued there till his death, in 1661; while John, the youngest of the family, became minister of Tarbolton, Ayrshire, from which he was ejected, for adherence to Presbytery, after the restoration of Charles II to the throne of Britain, and speedily sank under the hardships to which he was exposed, dying in the year 1669.

The superior genius of William, the eldest of this excellent band of brothers, was displayed in his early and successful attention to learning; but till his entrance into college life, he did not obtain that intimate and saving acquaintance with Divine truth which enabled him at once to stay his own soul upon God as the God of his salvation, and to prescribe most skilfully for the cases of spiritual disease that came under his notice. He felt himself greatly indebted for acquaintance with the way of holiness to the instructions of a near kinsman. This was his cousin, James Guthrie, then holding one of the chairs in the New College of St Andrews, and afterwards highly esteemed as the faithful minister of Stirling during the period of the Covenant, for his faithful adherence to which he obtained a martyr's crown. Samuel Rutherford, who became Professor of Divinity at St Andrews in 1639, took the guidance of William Guthrie's theological studies, confirmed and cherished the principles of piety already implanted, and brought him, with his whole soul, to devote himself to the service of Christ. That he might not be entangled in the network of earthly concerns, he resigned his estate at Pitforthy to a younger brother, not engaged at that time in the prosecution of sacred studies. Thus trained in the schools of literature, and rendered familiar with religion both in theory and practice, William Guthrie was well fitted for usefulness as a preacher of the gospel. He was licensed, with the high approbation of the Presbytery, in August 1642. It was fully two years later that he obtained a church in the newly erected parish of Fenwick; and was ordained minister, in compliance with the harmonious call of the people, in November 1644. His success and popularity were soon found to be great; and extended far beyond the Ayrshire district in which his parish lay – to Clydesdale, Stirling, and the Lothians. Several calls were addressed to him, but ineffectually, to quit his beloved people, till, about a year after his settlement, and very soon after his marriage to an excellent lady of the noble family of Loudon, he left them for a season, by appointment of the General Assembly, to attend the Scottish army as chaplain during the civil war that ended in the execution of Charles I, and the subjection of Scotland to the Protectorate of Cromwell.

While the Protector's troops kept possession of Glasgow about that time, William Guthrie's Christian heroism was called into exercise on a communion Sabbath in Andrew Gray's church. 'Several of the English officers had formed a design to put in execution the disorderly principle of a promiscuous admission to the Lord's table, by coming to it themselves without acquainting the minister, or being in a due manner found worthy of that privilege. Mr Guthrie, to whose share it fell to dispense the sacrament at that table, spoke to them, when they were leaving their pews in order to make their attempt, with such gravity, resolution, and zeal, that they were quite confounded, and sat down again without occasioning any further disturbance.'

The arrangements then made by the Church Courts regarding chaplains in the army, render it probable that he was relieved by his brethren at several intervals, and thus enjoyed occasionally the endearments of his home, and opportunities of pastoral and public usefulness. He was providentially preserved throughout the war, and returned to his flock with increased ardour and devotion. They needed his care; for at the commencement of his ministry, profanation of the Sabbath, desertion of the house of God, neglect of family religion, and gross ignorance, with a train of attendant evils, were prevalent among his parishioners. His talents, natural and acquired, were dexterously applied to check abounding iniquity. Let one instance suffice for illustration – that of a fowler in his parish engaging in his sport and deserting public worship on the Lord's day – a practice in which he had long indulged. 'Mr Guthrie asked him what was the reason he had for so doing? He told him that the Sabbath-day was the most fortunate day in all the week. Mr Guthrie asked him what he could make by that day's exercise? He replied that he could make half-a-crown. Mr Guthrie told him if he would go to church on Sabbath, he would give him as much; and by that means got his promise. After sermon was over, Mr Guthrie asked if he would come back the next Sabbath-day, and he would give him the same? which he did, and from that time afterwards never failed to keep the church. He afterwards became a member of his session.'

The stated calls made by Guthrie at the houses of his people were verv acceptable and profitable. The visitation of the sick and the dying, whom he never neglected, the instruction of the young in the doctrine that is according to godliness, and the ministrations of the pulpit, declared him a workman who needed not to be ashamed. As a consistent office-bearer, he duly attended to the government and discipline of the Church, in the session and superior judicatories. He seems to have been a member of the General Assembly of 1649, and stands in the lists of its Commission, along with such illustrious names as James Guthrie, the Marquis of Argyle, David Dickson, James Durham, and Samuel Rutherford.

During the unhappy division of the Church of Scotland into the parties of Resolutioners and Protesters or Remonstrants, the two Guthries, Samuel Rutherford, and several of the most pious and zealous Presbyterians, adhered to the latter; and Baillie mentions in his Letters, that at the meeting of their western synod, in 1654, 'the Remonstrants chose Mr William Guthrie for their Moderator.' His forbearance towards brethren taking the opposite side in that fatal schism has been acknowledged by his biographers; and his pastoral care was fully exercised. Ere long he published 'The Christian's Great Interest.' This work has gone through numerous editions, been translated into various languages, and continues to embalm his memory in the estimation of intelligent Christians of every name. The first edition of it appeared shortly before the restoration of Charles II.

Not long after the commencement of the persecution, Guthrie made one of his last efforts for the preservation of ecclesiastical freedom in the courts of the Church. This stand he took at a meeting of the Synod of Glasgow and Ayr, in April 1661, when he framed an address, designed for presentation to Parliament had the troubles of the time permitted, which the Synod approved of, as 'containing a faithful testimony of the purity of our reformation in worship, doctrine, discipline, and government, in terms equally remarkable for their prudence and their courage.' Two months later his zeal for the same cause was manifested by his earnest desire to attend, on the scaffold, his illustrious kinsman, James Guthrie, who sealed his testimony with his blood, in June 1661, at the cross of Edinburgh. His deference to the urgent entreaties of his session alone prevented him from engaging in so perilous a service. The respect which his affable deportment and able performance of pastoral duty gained for him from high and low screened him from persecution, and he persevered in preaching to his flock the truth as it is in Jesus. His intellectual powers and Christian experience were conspicuous in his discourses, and many, we believe, were the imperishable seals of his ministry, for it is averred by one of his contemporaries, Matthew Crawford, minister at Eastwood, that 'he converted and confirmed many thousand souls, and was esteemed the greatest practical preacher in Scotland.' Another of them declares his diligence and success among the people of Fenwick to have been so great, that almost all of them 'were brought to make a fair profession of godliness, and had the worship of God in their families. And it was well known that many of them were sincere, and not a few of them eminent Christians.' To the person who ejected him, he humbly yet boldly ascribed his great success to God: 'I thank Him for it; yea, I look upon it as a door which God opened to me for preaching this gospel, which neither you nor any man else was able to shut, till it was given you of God.' He was now called to experience those trials which had been delayed longer in his case than in that of most of his faithful brethren through the influence of the Earl of Glencairn, then Chancellor of Scotland, who both respected him as a man of worth, and recollected with gratitude Guthrie's kindness to him during an imprisonment to which the Earl had been subjected for his loyalty to the King during the sway of Cromwell.

Sabbath, the 24th of July, was fixed as the day for enforcing the decree. The people of Fenwick, greatly grieved at the prospect of losing so faithful a minister, observed the Wednesday preceding as a day of humiliation and prayer. Guthrie found an appropriate text for the occasion in these words of Hosea 13:9, 'O Israel, thou hast destroyed thyself'; solemnly inculcated on his flock patience and perseverance in the way of holiness, and appointed an early meeting of the congregation for the following Sabbath. The light of that day of the Son of Man ushered in a sorrowful morning for the people who then met to listen for the last time to the welcome voice of their beloved pastor. His theme, most suitable for the day, was the clause which followed his Wednesday's text, 'But in Me is thine help.' At the close of his sermon every countenance was suffused with tears, while he directed his hearers to the 'Fountain of help, when the gospel and ministers were taken from them; and took his leave of them, commending them to this great God, who was able to build them up, and help them in the time of their need.'

Before nine o'clock the congregation had dispersed, sorrowing exceedingly that they should listen to his persuasive discourses no more. No sound occurred to disturb the quiet of the hallowed day, till the tramp of horses was heard in the distance, and the troop soon appeared headed by a rider in black, the curate of Calder, whom a fee of five pounds had induced to give formal notice of the sentence of suspension. He observed the ceremony of preaching the church vacant in the presence of a congregation of soldiers and children. In the manse he was courteously received by Guthrie, who declared, in the presence of the officers of the party, his reason for submission to the sentence as not arising from respect to the prelate's authority, which had no weight with him, adding, 'Were it not for the reverence I owe to the civil magistrate, I would not cease from the exercise of my ministry for all that sentence.' The following passage formed part of his solemn reply to the Archbishop's message: 'I here declare, I think myself called by the Lord to the work of the ministry, and did forsake my nearest relations in the world, and give up myself to the service of the gospel in this place, having received a unanimous call from this parish, and being tried and ordained by the Presbytery; and I bless the Lord He hath given me some success, and a seal of my ministry upon the souls and consciences of not a few that are gone to heaven, and of some that are yet in the way to it.' His bodily health, but indifferent before, suffered a severe shock on this occasion; he preached no more in the parish; and about two months later retired to his paternal estate at Pitforthy, now become his possession in consequence of the death of a surviving brother. It was his but for a year of pain and sorrow, caused by a complication of diseases, and by the calamities that were befalling the Church and nation. He was attended during his last illness by visitors belonging to all parties, received kindly but faithfully the Episcopalian clergy who came to converse with him, and died full of faith in the glorious gospel he had preached, with the confident hope of complete redemption. His death occurred on the afternoon of Wednesdav, the 10th of October 1665. Two daughters of a family of six children survived him, one of whom became the wife of the Rev Patrick Warner, of Irvine, and mother of Margaret Warner, who was afterwards married to the Rev Robert Wodrow, of Eastwood, the faithful chronicler of the sufferings of the Church of Scotland.

None of Guthrie's sermons appear to have been published during his lifetime. As a specimen of the faithful and practical character of his preaching, we give an extract from a discourse long preserved among the Wodrow MSS, and recently printed, entitled, 'A Sermon on Sympathie.' The text is Matthew 15:23, 'Send her away, for she cryeth after us.' – 'Is it so that sympathie is so cold and weak among God's people at this time, when so much of it is called for? Then I would have yow drawing these three conclusions from it: 1. When any thing ails yow, pray much for yourself; I assure yow ye will get little help of others. 2. As yow would lippen little to other folk's prayers, so ye would make meikle use of Christ's intercession. These prayers are little worth that flow not from sympathie; and, 3. Reckon all your receipts to be free favour, and neither the return of your own or other folk's prayers. I do not forbid yow to pray yourself, nor to seek the help of other folk's prayers, nor do I judge yow or them void of sympathie; but I would have yow lippening less to them, and making more use of Christ and His intercession.'

Guthrie's theological tutor and bosom friend, Samuel Rutherford, thus expresses his regard for him and his flock during a season of public agitation: 'Dear Brother, help me, and get me the help of their prayers who are with you, in whom is my delight.' The author of 'The Christian's Great Interest' was also very highly esteemed by another of his illustrious contemporaries, Dr John Owen, who, on one occasion, drawing a little gilded copy of Guthrie's treatise from his pocket, said to a minister of the Church of Scotland, 'That author I take to have been one of the greatest divines that ever wrote; it is my *Vade-mecum*, and I carry it and the Sedan New Testament, still about with me. I have written several folios, but there is more divinity in it than in them all.'

Many years after the author's death, this work, with others of a similar nature, was instrumental in arousing to deeper concern for his soul's salvation, John Brown, then a shepherd boy in the neighbourhood of Abernethy, and afterwards highly distinguished as a minister of the gospel, and Professor of Divinity for nearly twenty years in one of the branches of the Secession Church. How many more may be the cases in which it has been blessed to the conviction, conversion, and edification of those whom it might enable to teach others also, the great day alone will declare. The following references to it, in the interesting Memoirs of Dr Chalmers, prove the high opinion he had formed of the genius it displays: 'Would you inquire for 'Guthrie's Trial of a Saving Interest in Christ? It is a small duodecimo; and has been long the favourite author of our peasantry in Scotland. He wrote about a hundred and fifty years ago; and one admirable property of his work is, that while it guides it purifies. It makes known all our defects, but ministers the highest comfort in the presence of a feeling of our defects. To find mercy we need only to feel misery.' . . . 'I am on the eve of finishing Guthrie, which I think is the best book I ever read. I shall leave it as a present to the Anster folks, and pass from it to 'Brook on

Religious Experience',' . . . 'I should like to know how the little book I left was relished among you. I still think it the best composition I ever read relating to a subject in which we are all deeply interested, and about which it is my earnest prayer, that we may all be found on the right side of the question.'

Having given the opinions of these eminent divines regarding the 'Christian's Great Interest,' we presume not to attempt a delineation of the merits of its excellent author. The wise and the good of his own day, as well as of subsequent times, have held him in grateful remembrance, and his works continue to minister blessing to the people of God.

PART I

The trial of a saving interest in Christ

Introduction

Since there are so many people living under the ordinances, pretending, without ground, to a special interest in Christ, and to His favour and salvation, as is clear from the words of our Lord – 'Many will say to Me in that day, Lord, Lord, have we not prophesied in Thy name, and in Thy name have cast out devils, and in Thy name done many wonderful works? And then will I profess unto them, I never knew you: depart from Me, ye that work iniquity.' [Matt 7:22, 23.] *'Afterward came also the other virgins, saying, Lord, Lord, open to us. But He answered and said, Verily I say unto you, I know you not.'* [Matt 25:11, 12.] *'Strive to enter in at the strait gate; for many, I say unto you, will seek to enter in, and shall not be able.'* [Luke 13:24.] – *and since many who have good ground of claim to Christ are not established in the confidence of His favour, but remain in the dark, without comfort, hesitating concerning the reality of godliness in themselves, and speaking little in the commendation of religion to others, especially in the time of their straits: I shall speak a little respecting two things of the greatest concern. The one is, How a person may know if he hath a true and special interest in Christ, and whether he doth lay just claim to God's favour and salvation. The other is, In case a person fall short of assurance in this trial, what course he should take for making sure of God's friendship and salvation to himself.*

QUESTION ONE

How shall a man know if he hath a true and special interest in Christ, and whether he hath, or may lay claim justly to, God's favour and salvation?

CHAPTER I

Things premised for the better understanding of the trial itself

Before we speak directly to the question, we shall premise some things, to make way for the answer.

I A MAN'S INTEREST IN CHRIST MAY BE KNOWN

First, That a man's interest in Christ, or his gracious state, may be known, and that with more certainty than people conjecture; yea, and the knowledge of it may be more easily attained unto than many imagine; for not only hath the Lord commanded men to know their interest in Him, as a thing attainable – 'Examine yourselves, whether ye be in the faith' [2 *Cor* 13:5]; 'Give diligence to make your calling and election sure' [2 *Peter* 1:10] – but many of the saints have attained unto the clear persuasion of their interest in Christ, and in God as their own God. How often do they call Him their God and their portion? and how persuaded is Paul 'that nothing can separate him from the love of God?' [*Rom* 8:38, 39.] Therefore the knowledge of a man's gracious state is attainable.

And this knowledge of it, which may be attained, is no fancy and mere conceit, but it is most sure: 'Doubtless Thou art our Father,' saith the prophet [*Is* 63:16], in name of the Church. It is clear from this: (1) That can be no fancy, but a very sure knowledge, which doth yield to a rational man comfort in most real straits; but so doth this – 'When the people spake of stoning David, he encouraged himself in the Lord his God.' [1 *Sam* 30:6.] He saith, 'He will not be afraid though ten thousands rise up against him.' [*Ps* 3:6.] Compare these words with the following: 'But Thou, O Lord, art a shield for me; my glory, and the lifter up of mine head.' [*Ps* 3:3.] 'The Lord is my light, and my salvation, whom shall I fear? the Lord is the strength of my life, of whom shall I be afraid? Though an host should encamp against me, my heart shall not fear; though war should rise against me, in this will I be confident.' [*Ps* 27: 1–3.]

2. That is a sure knowledge of a thing which maketh a wise merchant sell all he hath, that he may keep it sure; that maketh a man forego children, lands, life, and suffer the spoiling of all joyfully; but so doth this – *Matt* 13:44; *Mark* 10:28, 29; *Heb* 10:34; *Rom* 5:3; *Acts* 5:41.

3. That must be a sure and certain knowledge, and no fancy, upon which a man voluntarily and freely doth adventure his soul when he is stepping into eternity, with this word in his mouth, 'This is all my desire' [2 *Sam* 23:5]; but such a knowledge is this.

And again, not only may a godly man come to the sure knowledge of his gracious state, but it is more easily attainable than many apprehend: for supposing, what shall be afterwards proved, that a man may know the gracious work of God's Spirit in himself; if he will but argue rationally from thence, he shall be forced to conclude his interest in Christ, unless he deny clear Scripture truths. I shall only make use of one here, because we are to speak more directly to this afterwards. A godly man may argue thus, Whosoever receive Christ are justly reputed the children of God – 'But as many as received Him, to them gave He power to become the sons of God' [*John* 1:12]; but I have received Christ in all the ways which the word there can import: for I am pleased with the device of salvation by Christ, I agree to the terms, I welcome the offer of Christ in all His offices, as a King to rule over me, a Priest to offer sacrifice and intercede for me, a Prophet to teach me; I lay out my heart for Him and towards Him, resting on Him as I am able. What else can be meant by the word RECEIVING? Therefore may I say, and conclude plainly and warrantably, I am justly to reckon myself God's child, according to the aforesaid scripture, which cannot fail.

2 TO BE SAVINGLY IN COVENANT WITH GOD IS OF THE HIGHEST IMPORTANCE

The *second* thing to be premised is, That a man be savingly in covenant with God is a matter of the highest importance: 'It is his life.' [*Deut* 32:47.] And yet very few have, or seek after a saving interest in the covenant; and many foolishly think they have such a thing without any solid ground. [*Matt* 7:14.] Few find, or walk in, the narrow way. This should alarm people to be serious about the matter, since it is of so great consequence to be in Christ, and since there be but few that may lay just claim to Him; and yet many do foolishly fancy an interest in Him, who are deceived by a false confidence, as the foolish virgins were. [*Matt* 25.]

3 WE MUST ALLOW OUR STATE TO BE DETERMINED BY SCRIPTURE

The *third* thing to be premised is, Men must resolve to be determined by Scripture in this matter of their interest in Christ. The Spirit speaking in the Scripture is judge of all controversies – 'To the law and to the testimony; if they speak not according to this word, it is because there is no light in them' [*Is* 8:20] – and of this also, whether a man be savingly in covenant with God or not. Therefore do not mock God whilst you seem to search after such a thing. If we prove from Scripture, which is the uncontroverted rule, that you are gracious, and have made a covenant savingly with God, then resolve to grant so much, and to acquiesce in it; and if the contrary appear, let there be a determination of the controversy, else you do but *mock* the Lord, and so 'your bands shall be made strong' [*Is* 28:22]; for 'a jot of His word cannot fail.' [*Matt* 5:11.] Therefore, seek eye-salve from Christ to judge of things according as the word of God shall discover them to be.

4 REASONS WHY SO FEW ATTAIN TO A DISTINCT KNOWLEDGE OF THEIR INTEREST IN CHRIST

The *fourth* thing to be premised is, Although the matter of a man's interest in Christ be of so great importance, and the way to attain to the knowledge of it so plainly held forth in the Scriptures, yet there be but few who reach the distinct knowledge of it. And that this may not discourage any person from attempting it, I shall hint some few reasons why so few come to the clear knowledge of it; which will also prepare the way for what is to be spoken afterwards.

[1] *Ignorance of God and His ways*

The *first* thing which hinders many from the knowledge of their interest in Christ is their ignorance of some special principles of religion; as

1. That it was free love in God's bosom, and nothing in man, that moved Him to send a Saviour to perfect the work of redemption – 'God so loved the world, that He gave His only begotten Son.' [*John* 3:16.] Men are still seeking some ground for that work in themselves, which leads away from suitable and high apprehensions of the first spring and rise of God's covenant favour to His people, which hath no reason, cause, or motive in us; and so they cannot come to the knowledge of their interest.

2. They are ignorant how that love effectually discovers itself to a man's heart, so as he hath ground to lay claim to it, namely, That ordinarily, *first*, It discovers his fallen state in himself, because of sin and corruption defiling the whole man, and any thing in him that might be called a righteousness: 'All these things are loss and dung.' [*Phil* 3:8.] *Secondly*, It discovers Christ as the full and satisfying treasure, above all things: 'The man finds a treasure, for which with joy he selleth all that he hath.' [*Matt* 13:44, 46.] *Thirdly*, It determines the heart, and causes it to approach unto a living God in the ordinances: 'Blessed is the man whom Thou choosest, and causest to approach unto Thee, that he may dwell in Thy courts' [*Ps* 65:4]; and causeth the heart to wait upon Him, and Him alone: 'My soul, wait thou only upon God.' [*Ps* 62:5.] Thus having dropped in the seed of God in the heart, and formed Christ there [*Gal* 4:19], the heart is changed and made new in the work [*Ezek* 36:26]; and God's law is so stamped upon the heart in that change [*Jer* 31:33], that the whole yoke of Christ is commended to the man without exception. [*Rom* 7:12, 16.] The law is acknowledged good, holy, just, and spiritual. Upon all which, from that new principle of life, there flow out acts of a new life – [*Gal* 5:6], 'Faith worketh by love'; [*Rom*

6:18, 22], and the man becometh a servant of righteousness unto God, which especially appears in the spirituality of worship: men then 'serve God in spirit and in truth, in the newness of the spirit, and not in the oldness of the letter' [*John* 4:24; *Rom* 7:6] – and tenderness in all manner of conversation. The man then 'exerciseth himself how to keep a conscience void of offence towards God and towards men.' [*Acts* 24:16.] Now in this way doth the love of God discover itself unto man, and acteth on him, so as he hath ground of laying some good claim to it; and so as he may justly think that the love which sent a Saviour had respect to such a man as hath had these things made out unto him. Surely ignorance in this doth hinder many from the knowledge of their interest in Christ; for if a man know not how God worketh with a person, so as he may justly lay claim to His love, which was from eternity, he will wander in the dark, and not come to the knowledge of an interest in Him.

3. Many are also ignorant of this, that God alone is the hope of His people; He is called 'the hope of Israel.' [*Jer* 14:8.] Although inherent qualifications are evidences of it, yet the staying of the heart upon Him, as a full blessing and satisfying portion, is faith – 'The faith and hope must be in God' [1 *Peter* 1:21] – and the only proper condition which giveth right to the saving blessings of the covenant: 'To him that worketh not but believeth, faith is counted for righteousness.' [*Rom* 4:5.] Indeed, if any person take liberty here, and turn grace unto licentiousness, there is, without doubt, in so far a delusion: since there is mercy with Him upon condition that it conciliate fear to him. [*Ps* 130:4.] Yea, hardly can any man who hath found the former-mentioned expressions of God's love made out in him, make a cloak of the covenant for sinful liberty, with-

out some measure of a spiritual conflict. In this respect, 'he that is born of God doth not sin,' and 'he who doth so sin hath not seen God.' [1 *John* 3:6, 9.] I say God is the hope of His people, and not their own holiness. If they intend honestly and long seriously to be like unto Him, many failings should not weaken their hope and confidence, for it is in Him 'who changeth not' [*Mal* 3:6]; 'and if any man sin, we have an advocate.' [1 *John* 2:1.] Now, when men place their hope in any other thing besides the Lord, it is no wonder they are kept in a staggering condition, according to the changes of the thing which they make the ground of their hope; since they give not to God the glory due to His name, and which He will not give to another. 'They who know Thy name will put their trust in Thee.' [*Ps* 9:10.] 'My glory will I not give to another: I am the Lord, that is my name.' [*Is* 42:8.]

4. Many are ignorant of the different ways and degrees of God's working with His people, and this doth much darken their knowledge and reflex acts of their interest in Him. This ignorance consists mainly of three things: (1) They are ignorant of the different degrees and ways of that work of the law, by which God ordinarily dealeth with men, and of the different ways in which the Lord bringeth people at first to Christ. They consider not that the jailer is not kept an hour in bondage [*Acts* 16]; Paul is kept in suspense three days [*Acts* 9]; Zaccheus not one moment [*Luke* 19]. (2) They are ignorant of, at least they do not consider, how different are the degrees of sanctification in the saints, and the honourable appearances thereof before men in some, and the sad blemishes thereof in others. Some are very blameless, and more free of gross outbreakings, adorning their profession much, as Job and

Zacharias. These are said to be 'perfect and upright, fearing God, and eschewing evil' [*Job* 1:8]; 'righteous before God, walking in all the commandments and ordinances of the Lord blameless.' [*Luke* 1:6.] Others were subject to very gross and sad evils, as Solomon, Asa, etc. (3) They are ignorant of the different communications of God's face and expressions of His presence. Some walk much in the light of God's countenance, and are much in sensible fellowship with Him, as David was; others are 'all their days kept in bondage, through fear of death.' [*Heb* 2:15.] Surely the ignorance of the different ways of God's working and dealing with His people doth very much darken the knowledge of their interest in Him, whilst they usually limit the Lord to one way of working, which He doth not keep, as we have shown in the former examples.

[2] *Dealing deceitfully with God and their own consciences*

The *second* thing which darkens men about their interest in Christ is, There is one thing or other wherein their heart, in some respect, doth condemn them, as dealing deceitfully and guilefully with God. It is not to be expected that those can come to clearness about their interest, whose heart doth condemn them for keeping up some known transgressions against the Lord, which they will not let go, neither are using the means which they know to be appointed by God for delivering them from it: Neither can those come to clearness who know some positive duty commanded them in their stations, which they deceitfully shift and shun, not closing cheerfully with it, or not willing to be led into it. These are also, in some respects, condemned of their own heart, as the former sort are; and in that case it is difficult to come to a distinct knowledge of their state: 'If our heart condemn us not, then have we confidence toward God.' [1 *John* 3:21.] It is supposed here, that a self-condemning heart maketh void a man's confidence proportionally before God.

I do not deny but that men may on good grounds plead an interest in Christ in the case of prevailing iniquity: 'Iniquities prevail against me; as for our transgressions, Thou shalt purge them away.' [*Ps* 65:3.] 'I see another law in my members warring against the law of my mind, and bringing me into captivity to the law of sin which is in my members. O wretched man that I am, who shall deliver me from the body of this death? I thank God through Jesus Christ our Lord. So then, with the mind I myself serve the law of God, but with the flesh the law of sin.' [*Rom* 7:23, 24.] But it is hard to be attained, if at all attainable, when the heart is dealing deceitfully, and entertaining known guile in any particular: therefore, let people clear themselves of the particular, which they know too well. It is the thing which hinders them, marring their confidence and access in all their approaches unto God. 'Yet ye have forsaken Me, and served other gods: wherefore I will deliver you no more.' [*Judges* 10:13.] The idolatries of the people are cast up to them by the Lord, and their suit rejected thereupon. That which draweth away the heart first in the morning, and last at night, like 'an oven heated at night, and it burneth as a flaming fire in the morning' [*Hos* 7:6], spoken of the wicked; and taketh up their thoughts often on their bed: as it is said of some, 'He deviseth mischief upon his bed' [*Ps* 36:4]: That which doth ordinarily lead away the heart in time of religious duty, and the remembrance of which hath power to enliven and quicken the spirits more than the remembrance of God, so as 'their heart is after the heart of some detestable thing' [*Ezek* 11:21]: That which withstandeth men when they would lay hold on the promise, as God casteth up men's sins to them who are meddling with His covenant, 'What hast thou to do to declare My statutes, or that thou shouldest take My covenant in thy mouth?' [*Ps* 50:16]: *that* is the thing which doth prevent the knowledge of a gracious state. Let it go, and it will be more easy to reach the knowledge of an interest in Christ.

[3] *Slothfulness and Negligence*

The *third* thing which hindereth in many the knowledge of an interest in Christ is, A spirit of sloth and careless negligence. They complain that they know not whether they be in Christ or not; but as few take pains to be in Him, so few take pains to try if they be in Him. It is a work and business which cannot be done sleeping: 'Examine yourselves whether ye be in the faith; prove your own selves: know ye not your own selves.' [2 *Cor* 13:5.] The several words used here, namely, *Examine*, *prove*, *know* – intimate that there is a labour in it: Diligence must be used to make our 'calling and election sure.' [2 *Peter* 1:10.] It is a business above flesh and blood: the holy 'anointing which teacheth all things,' must make us 'know the things freely given to us of God.' [1 *John* 2:27.] Shall the Lord impart a business of so great concernment, and not so much as 'be inquired after to do it for men?' [*Ezek* 36:37.] Be ashamed, you who spend so much time in reading of romances, in adorning your persons, in hawking and hunting, in consulting the law concerning your outward state in the world, and it may be in worse things than these; Be ashamed, you that spend so little time in the search of this, whether ye be an heir of glory or not? whether you be in the way that leadeth to heaven, or that way which will land you in darkness for ever? You who judge this below you, and unworthy of your pains, any part or minute of your time, it is probable, in God's account, you have judged yourselves *unworthy of everlasting life*, so that you shall have no lot with God's people in this matter.

[4] *Their having no fixed idea of what evidence would satisfy them*

The *fourth* thing that darkens the knowledge of an interest in Christ is, Men do not condescend upon what would satisfy them. They complain that God will not show unto them what He is about to do with them, but yet cannot say they know what would satisfy them concerning His purpose. This is a sad thing. Shall we think those are serious who have never as yet pitched on what would satisfy them, nor are making earnest inquiry after what should satisfy? If the Lord had left us in the dark in that matter, we were less inexcusable; but since the grounds of satisfaction, and the true marks of an interest in Christ, are so clear and frequent in Scripture, and so 'many things written, that our joy may be full' [1 *John* 1:4]; and, 'that those who believe,' may 'know that they have eternal life' [1 *John* 5:13]; and since 'he that believeth hath the witness of it in himself' [1 *John* 5:10], none can pretend excuse here. We shall not here insist to show what may and should satisfy concerning our interest, since we are to speak directly of it afterwards.

[5] *Their dependence on changeable evidence*

The *fifth* thing that helps much to keep men in the dark with respect to their interest in Christ is, They pitch upon some mutable grounds, which are not so apposite proofs of the truth of an interest in Christ as of the comfortable state of a triumphing soul sailing before the wind; and marks which I grant are precious in themselves, and do make out an interest clearly where they are; yet they are such as without which an interest in Christ may be, and be known also in a good measure. We shall touch on a few of them.

First, Some think that all who have a true interest in Him are above the prevailing power of every sin; but this is contrary to that of *Ps* 65:3, 'Iniquities prevail against me; as for our transgressions, Thou shalt purge them away;' where we find that holy man laying just claim to pardon, in the case of prevailing iniquity; and that of *Rom* 7:23, 24, 25, where Paul thanketh God through Christ, as freed from the condemnation of the law, even whilst a law in his members leadeth captive unto sin.

Secondly, Some think that all true saints have constantly access to God in prayer, and sensible returns of prayer at all times; but this is contrary to the many sad exercises of His people, complaining often that they are not heard nor regarded of God: 'How long wilt Thou forget me, O Lord? for ever? how long wilt Thou hide Thy face from me?' [*Ps* 13:1]; 'My God, my God, why hast Thou forsaken me? why art Thou so far from helping me, and from the words of my roaring? O my God, I cry in the day time, but Thou hearest not; and in the night season, and am not silent.' [*Ps* 22:1, 2.]

Thirdly, Some think that all who have any true interest in Him have God witnessing the same unto them, by a high operation of that *witnessing Spirit* of His, spoken of: 'The Spirit itself beareth witness with our spirit that we are the children of God' [*Rom* 8:16, whereof afterwards];

and so they still suspect their own interest in Christ, because of the want of this. But they do not remember that they must first believe and give credit to that record which God hath given of His Son, that there is life enough in Him for men [1 *John* 5:10, 11], and then look for the seal and witness of the Spirit: 'In whom, after ye believed, ye were sealed with that Holy Spirit of promise.' [*Eph* 1:13.] As long as people hold fast these principles, and the like, they can hardly come to the knowledge of their gracious state, which God hath warranted people to prove and clear up to themselves, otherways than by these aforesaid things.

5 SOME MISTAKES CONCERNING AN INTEREST IN CHRIST REMOVED

The *fifth* thing to be premised is, The removal of some mistakes into which people may readily run themselves when they are about to prove their interest in Christ; as –

1. It is a mistake to think that every one who is in Christ doth know that he is in Him; for many are truly gracious, and have a good title to eternal life, who do not know so much, until it be made out afterwards: 'These things are written to them that believe, that they may know they have a title to eternal life' [1 *John* 5:13]; that is, that they may know they are believers, and so it is supposed they knew it not before.

2. It is a mistake to think that all who come to the knowledge of their interest in Christ do attain an equal certainty about it. One may say, 'He is persuaded nothing present, or to come, can separate him from the love of God' [*Rom* 8:38]; another cometh but this length, 'Lord, I believe, help my unbelief.' [*Mark* 9:24.]

3. It is a mistake to think that every one who attains a strong persuasion of his interest doth always hold there; for he who to-day may say of the Lord, 'He is his refuge' [*Ps* 91:2], and 'his portion' [*Ps* 119:57], will at another time say, 'He is cut off' [*Ps* 31:22], and will ask, 'if the truth of God's promise doth fail for evermore?' [*Ps* 77:7, 8, 9.]

4. It is also a mistake to think that every one who attains a good knowledge of his gracious state can formally answer all objection made to the contrary; but yet they may hold fast the conclusion, and say, 'I know whom I have believed.' [2 *Tim* 1:12.] There are few grounds of the Christian religion, whereof many people are so persuaded, as that they are able to maintain them formally against all arguments brought to the contrary; and yet they may and will hold the conclusion steadfastly and justly; so it is in the case in hand.

5. It is no less a mistake to imagine, that the vain groundless confidence, which many profane ignorant atheists do maintain, is this knowledge of an interest in Christ which we plead for. Many do falsely avow Him 'to be their Father' [*John* 8:41]; and many look for heaven, who are beguiled, like the 'foolish virgins.' [*Matt* 25:12.] Yet we must not think, because of this, that all knowledge of an interest is a delusion and fancy, although these fools be deceived; for, whilst thousands are deluded, some can say on good and solid grounds, 'We know that we are of God, and that the whole world lieth in wickedness.' [1 *John* 5:19.]

CHAPTER II

The various ways by which men are drawn to Christ

Having premised these things, it now follows that we give some marks by which a man may know if he be savingly in covenant with God, and hath a special interest in Christ, so that he may warrantably lay claim to God's favour and salvation. We shall only pitch upon two great and principal marks, not willing to trouble people with many.

SECTION I

Some are drawn without a conscious preparatory work of the law

But before we begin to these, we will speak of a preparatory work of the law, of which the Lord doth ordinarily make use, to prepare His own way in men's souls. This may have its own weight as a mark, with some persons. It is called the Work of the Law, or the Work of Humiliation. It hath some relation to that 'spirit of bondage,' and doth now under the New Testament answer unto it, and usually leadeth on to the 'Spirit of adoption.' [*Rom* 8:15.]

Only here, let it be remembered – (1) That we are not to speak of this preparatory work of the law as a negative mark of a true interest in Christ, as if none might lay claim to God's favour who have not had this preparatory work, in its several steps, as we are to speak of it; for, as we shall see, the Lord does not always observe the same plan with men. (2) The great reason why we speak of it is, because the Lord deals with many, whom He effectually calls by some such preparatory work; and to those, who have been so dealt with, it may prove strengthening, and will confirm them in laying more weight on the marks which follow. (3) It may help to encourage others, who are under such bondage of spirit, as a good indication of a gracious work to follow; for, as we shall point out, it will be rarely found to miscarry and fail of a gracious issue. (4) Where God uses such a preparatory work, He doth not keep one way or measure in it, as we shall see.

For the more distinct handling of this preparatory work, we shall shortly hint the most ordinary ways by which the Lord leads people savingly into His covenant, and draws them unto Christ.

1 SOME ARE CALLED FROM THE WOMB

There are some called from the womb, as John the Baptist was [*Luke* 1]; or in very early years, before they can be actively engaged in Satan's ways, as Timothy. [2 *Tim* 3:15.] It cannot be supposed that these have such a preparatory work as we are to speak of. And because some persons may pretend to this way of effectual calling, we offer these marks of it, whereby those who have been so called may be confirmed.

1. Such are usually from their childhood kept free from ordinary pollutions, as swearing, lying, mocking of religion and religious persons, etc., with which children are often defiled. Those whom God calleth effectually, He sanctifieth from the time of that effectual calling: 'Sin cannot have dominion over them,' as over others, 'Because they are under grace.' [*Rom* 6:14.]

2. Religion is, as it were, natural to them; I mean, they need not to be much pressed to religious duties even when they are but children; they run willingly that way, because there is an inward principle of 'love constraining them' [2 *Cor* 5:14], so that they yield themselves servants of righteousness, without outward constraint. [*Rom* 6:16.]

3. Although such know not when they were first acquainted with God, yet they have afterwards such exercises of spirit befalling them as the saints in Scripture, of whose first conversion we are not told. They are, upon some occasions, shut out from God, and are again admitted, in their apprehension, to come near; their heart is also further broken up by the ordinances, as is said of Lydia. [*Acts* 16:14.] And ordinarily they remember when some special subject of religion and duty, or when some sin, of which they were not taking notice before, was discovered to them. They who can apply these things to themselves, have much to say for their effectual calling from their youth.

2 SOME ARE CALLED IN MATURE LIFE, IN A SOVEREIGN GOSPEL-WAY

Some are brought to Christ in a sovereign gospel-way, when the Lord, by some few words of love swallowing up any work of the law, quickly taketh a person prisoner at the first, as He did Zaccheus [*Luke* 19], and others, who, upon a word spoken by Christ, did leave all and follow Him; and we hear nothing of a law-work dealing with them before they close with Christ Jesus.

And because some may pretend to this way of calling, we shall touch on some things most remarkable in that transaction with Zaccheus, for their clearing and confirmation. (1) He had some desire to see Christ, and such a desire as made him waive that which some would have judged prudence and discretion, whilst he climbeth up a tree that he might see Him. (2) Christ spake to his heart, and that word took such hold upon him, that presently with joy he accepted Christ's offer, and closed with Christ as Lord, whilst few of any note were following Him. (3) Upon this his heart was opened to the poor; although it seems he was a covetous man before. (4) He had a due impression of his former ways, evidencing his respect to the law of Moses, and this he signifies before all the company then present, not shrinking from taking shame to himself in such things as probably were notorious to the world. (5) Upon all these things, Christ confirms and ratifies the contract by His word; recommending to him that oneness of interest which behoved to be between him and the saints, and the thoughts of his own lost condition, if Christ had not come and sought him; all which is clear from *Luke* 19:3–10.

We grant the Lord calleth some so; and if any can lay claim to the special things we have now hinted, they have a good confirmation of God's dealing with them from Scripture; neither are they to vex themselves because of the want of a distinct preparatory law work, if their heart hath yielded unto Christ; for a work of the law is not desirable, except for this end. Therefore Christ offers Himself directly in the Scripture, and people are invited to come to Him; and although many will not come to Him who is the Surety, until the spirit of bondage distress them for their debt, yet if any, upon the knowledge of their lost estate, would flee and yield to Christ, none might warrantably press a work of the law upon them.

As for others, whom Christ persuaded by a word to

follow Him, whatsoever He did, or howsoever He spake to them, at His first meeting with them, we must rationally suppose that then He discovered to them so much of their necessity, and His own fullness and excellency, as made them quit all, and run after Him; and if He do so to any, we crave no more, since there is room enough there for the Physician.

So that from all this, as some may be confirmed and strengthened, with whom God hath so dealt, so there is no ground for deluded souls to flatter themselves in their condition, who remain ignorant and senseless of their own miseries, and Christ's all-sufficiency, and hold fast deceit.

3 SOME ARE GRACIOUSLY CALLED AS DEATH APPROACHES

There are some brought in to Christ in a way yet more declarative of His free grace; and this is, when He effectually calls men at the hour of death. We find somewhat recorded of this way in that pregnant example of the 'thief on the cross.' [*Luke* 23:39–45.] Although this seems not very pertinent for the purpose in hand, yet we shall speak a little of it, that, on the one hand, men may be sparing to judge and pass sentence on either themselves or others before the last breath; and we shall, on the other hand, speak so particularly, that none may dare to delay so great a business to the last hour of their life.

We find these remarkable circumstances in the conversation between Christ and the thief. (1) The man falls out with his former companion. (2) He dares not speak a wrong word of God, whose hand is on him, but justifies Him in all that has befallen him. (3) He now sees Jesus Christ persecuted by the world without a cause, and mos injuriously. (4) He discovers Christ to be a Lord and a King, whilst His enemies seem to have Him under. (5) He believes a state of glory after death so really, that he prefers a portion of it to the present safety of his bodily life, which he knew Christ was able to grant him at that time, and he might have chosen that with the other thief. (6) Although he was much abased in himself, and so humbled that he pleaded but that Christ would remember him, yet he was nobly daring to throw himself upon the covenant, on life and death; and he had so much faith of Christ's all-sufficiency, that he judged a simple remembrance from Christ would supply all his need. (7) He acquiesced sweetly in the word which Christ spake to him for the ground of his comfort. All which are very clear in the case of that poor dying man, and prove a real work of God upon his heart.

As this example may encourage some to wait for good from God, who cannot as yet lay clear claim to any gracious work of His Spirit; so we entreat all, as they love their souls, not to delay their souls' salvation, hoping for such assistance from Christ in the end, as too many do; – this being a rare miracle of mercy, in which Christ honourably triumphed over the ignominy of His cross; a parallel to which we shall hardly find in all the Scripture besides. Yea, as there be but few at all saved: 'Many be called, but few are chosen' [*Matt* 20:16]; and fewest saved this way; so the Lord hath peremptorily threatened to laugh at the calamity, and not to hear the cry of such as mocked formerly at His reproof, and would not hear when He called to them: 'Because I have called, and ye refused, I have stretched out my hand, and no man regarded; but ye have set at nought all my counsel, and would none of my reproof; I also will laugh at your calamity, I will mock when your fear cometh' [*Prov* 1:24–26]: which scripture, although it doth not shut mercy's door upon any, who at the hour of death do sincerely judge themselves and flee to Christ, as this penitent thief did; yet it certainly implieth that very few, who reject the offer until then, are honoured with repentance as he was; and so their cry, as not being sincere, and of the right stamp, shall not be heard.

SECTION II
Men are ordinarily prepared for Christ by the work of the Law

The most ordinary way by which many are brought to Christ, is by a clear and discernible work of the law, and humiliation; which we generally call *the spirit of bondage*, as was hinted before. We do not mean that every one, whose conscience is awakened with sin and fear of wrath, does really close with Christ; the contrary appears in Cain, Saul, Judas, etc. But there is a conviction of sin, an awakening of conscience, and work of humiliation, which, as we shall point out, rarely miscarries, or fails of a gracious issue, but ordinarily doth resolve into the Spirit of adoption, and a gracious work of God's Spirit. And because the Lord deals with many sinners this way, and we find that many are much puzzled about giving judgment of this law-work, we shall speak of it particularly.

This work is either more violent and sudden, or it is more quiet and gradual, so as to be protracted through a greater length of time, by which means the steps of it are very discernible. It is more violent in some, as in the jailer, Paul, and some other converts in the book of the Acts of the Apostles, on whom Christ did break in at an instant, and fell on them as with fire and sword, and led them captive terribly. And because some great legal shakings are deceitful, and turn to nothing, if not worse, we shall point at some things remarkable in these converts spoken of before, which proves the work of the law on them to have had a gracious issue and result. (1) Some word of truth or dispensation puts the person to a dreadful stand, with a great stir in the soul; some 'are pricked in heart' [*Acts* 2:37]; some fall a 'trembling.']*Acts* 16:29.] And thus it is, that the person is brought to his wits' end: 'What wilt Thou have me to do? 'saith Paul. [*Acts* 9:6.] 'What must I do to be saved?' saith the jailer. [*Acts* 16:30.] (2) The person is content to have salvation and God's friendship on any terms, as the question implies, 'What shall I do?' As if he had said, What would I not do? what would I not forego? what would I not undergo? (3) The person accepts the condition offered by Christ and His servants, as is clear in the fore-cited scriptures. (4) The person presently becomes of one interest with the saints, joins himself with that persecuted society, puts respect on those whom he had formerly persecuted, joining and continuing with them in the profession of Christ at all hazards. Those with whom the Lord hath so dealt, have much to say for a gracious work of God's Spirit in them: and it is probable many of them can date their work from such a particular time and word, or dispensation, and can give some account of what passed between God and them, and of a sensible change following in them from that time forward, as Paul giveth a good account of the work and way of God with him afterwards. [*Acts* 22.]

Again, the Lord sometimes carries on this work more calmly, softly, and gradually, protracting it so that the several steps of men's exercise under it are very discernible.

It would lead us to a great length to enlarge upon every step of it. We shall touch on the most observable things in it.

1. The Lord lays siege to men, who, it may be, have often refused to yield to Him, when offering Himself in the ordinances; and by some word preached, read, or borne in on the mind, or by some providence leading on unto the word, He doth assault the house kept peaceably by the strong man, the devil; and thus Christ, who is the stronger man, cometh upon him [*Luke* 11:22]; and by the Spirit of truth, fastens the word on the man, in which God's curse is denounced against such and such sins, of which the man knoweth himself guilty. The Spirit convinces the man, and binds it upon him, that he is the same person against whom the word of God speaks, because he is guilty of sins; and from some sins the man is led on to see more, until usually he comes to see the sins of his youth, sins of omission, etc.! yea, he is led on, until he sees himself guilty almost of the breach of the whole law: he sees 'innumerable evils compassing him,' as David speaks. [*Ps* 40:12.] A man sometimes will entertain alarming views of sin in this case, and is sharp-sighted to perceive himself guilty of almost every sin. Thus the Spirit cometh and convinceth of sin. [*John* 16:8.]

2. The Lord overcomes a special stronghold in the garrison, a refuge of lies, to which the man betaketh himself when his sins are thus discovered to him. The poor man pretends to faith in Christ, whereby he thinks his burden is taken off him, as the Pharisees said, 'We have one Father, even God.' [*John* 8:41.] They pretend to a special relation to God as a common Lord. The Spirit of God drives the man from this by the truth of the Scriptures, proving that he hath no true faith, and so no interest in

Christ, nor any true saving grace, showing clearly the difference between true grace and the counterfeit fancies which the man hath in him; and between him and the truly godly: as Christ laboureth to do with the Jews in *John* 8:42, 44 – 'If God were your Father, ye would love Me. Ye are of the devil, for ye do the lusts of your father.' So, 'fear surpriseth the hypocrite in heart' [*Is* 33:14]; especially when the Lord discovereth to him conditions, in many of those promises in which he trusted most, not easily attainable. He now seeth grace and faith to be another thing than once he judged them. We may in some respect apply that word here, The Spirit 'convinceth him of sin, because he hath not believed on the Son.' [*John* 16:9.] He is particularly convinced of unbelief: he now sees a vast difference between himself and the godly, who, he thought before, outstripped him only in some unnecessary, proud, hateful preciseness: he now sees himself deluded, and in the broad way with the perishing multitude: and so, in this sight of his misery, coucheth down under his own burden, which before this time he thought Christ did bear for him: he now begins to be alarmed as to the promises, because of such passages of Scripture as, 'What hast thou to do to take my covenant in thy mouth?' etc. [*Ps* 50:16.]

3. The man becomes careful about his salvation, and begins to take it to heart as the one thing necessary. He is brought to say with the jailer, 'What shall I do to be saved?' [*Acts* 16.] His salvation becomes the leading thing with him. It was least in his thoughts before, but now it prevails, and other things are much disregarded by him. Since his soul is ready to perish, 'what shall it profit him to gain the world, if he lose his soul?' [*Matt* 16:26.] Some here are much puzzled with the thoughts of an

irrevocable decree to their prejudice, and with the fears of uncertain death, which may attack them before their great concern is secured; and some are vexed with apprehensions that they are guilty of the sin against the Holy Ghost, which is unpardonable, and so are driven a dangerous length – Satan still reminding them of many sad examples of people who have miserably put an end to their own lives: but they are in the hand of one who 'knoweth how to succour them that are tempted.' [*Heb* 2:18.]

4. When a man is thus in hazard of miscarrying, the Lord useth a work of preventing mercy towards him, quietly and underhand supporting him; and this is by infusing into his mind the possibility of his salvation, leading him to the remembrance of numerous proofs of God's free and rich grace, in pardoning gross transgressors, such as Manasseh, who was a bloody idolatrous man, and had correspondence with the devil, and yet obtained mercy [2 *Chron* 33:11, 13]; and other scriptures bearing offers of grace and favour indifferently to all who will yield to Christ, whatsoever they have been formerly; so that the man is brought again to this – 'What shall I do to be saved?' which supposes that he apprehends a possibility of being saved, else he would not propound the question. He applies that or the like word to himself, 'It may be ye shall be hid in the day of the Lord's anger.' [*Zeph* 2:3.] He finds nothing excluding him from mercy now, if he have a heart for the thing. The man doth not, it may be, here perceive that it is the Lord who upholdeth him, yet afterwards he can say that, 'when his foot was slipping, God's mercy held him up,' as the Psalmist speaks in another case. [*Ps* 94:17, 18.] And he will afterwards say, when he 'was as a beast, and a fool, in many respects, God held him by the hand.' [*Ps* 73:22, 23.]

5. After this discovery of a possibility to be saved, there is a work of desire quickened in the soul; which is clear from that same expression, 'What shall I do to be saved?' But sometimes this desire is expressed amiss, whilst it goeth out thus, 'What shall I do that I may work the works of God?' [*John* 6:28.] In this case the man, formerly perplexed with fear and care about his salvation, would be at some work of his own to extricate himself; and here he suddenly resolves to do all that is commanded, and to forego every evil way (yet much misunderstanding Christ Jesus), and so begins to take some courage to himself, 'going about to establish his own righteousness, but not submitting unto the righteousness of God.' [*Rom* 10:3.] Whereupon the Lord makes a new assault upon him, intending the discovery of his absolutely fallen state in himself, that so room may be made for the Surety: as Joshua did to the people, when he found them so bold in their undertakings: 'Ye cannot serve the Lord,' saith he, 'for He is a holy God, a jealous God.' [*Josh* 24.] In this new assault the Lord – (1) Shows the man the spirituality of the law; the commandment cometh with a new charge in the spiritual meaning of it. [*Rom* 7:9.] 'The law came,' saith Paul, that is, in the spiritual meaning of it. Paul had never entertained such a view of the law before. (2) God most holily looseth the restraining bonds which he had laid upon the man's corruption, and suffereth it not only to boil and swell within, but to threaten to break out in all the outward members. Thus sin grows bold, and spurns at the law, becoming exceedingly sinful. 'But sin, taking occasion by the commandment, wrought in me all manner of concupiscence. For without the law, sin was dead. For I was alive without the law once; but when the commandment came, sin revived, and I died.

Was then that which is good made death unto me? God forbid. But sin, that it might appear sin, working death in me by that which is good; that sin by the commandment might become exceeding sinful.' [*Rom* 7:8–13.] (3) The Lord discovers to the man, more than ever, the uncleanness of his righteousness, and the spots of his best things. These things kill the man, and he dieth in his own conceit [*Rom* 7:9], and despaireth of relief in himself, if it come not from another source.

6. After many ups and downs, here ordinarily the man resolves on retirement; he desires to be alone, he cannot keep company as before. Like those in a besieged city, who, when they see they cannot hold out, and would be glad of any good condition from the besieging enemy, go to a council, that they may resolve on something; so the man here retires that he may speak with himself. This is like that 'communing with our own heart.' [*Ps* 4:4.] Thus God leadeth into the wilderness, that He may speak to the heart. [*Hos* 2:14.] When the person is retired, the thoughts of his heart, which were scattered in former steps of the exercise, do more observably throng in here. We shall reduce them to this method: (1) The man thinks of his unhappy folly in bearing arms against God; and here he dwells at large on his former ways, with a blushing countenance and self-loathing: 'Then shall ye remember your own evil ways, and your doings that were not good, and shall loathe yourselves in your own sight' [*Ezek* 36:31]; like that of *Psalm* 51:3, 'His sin is ever before him.' (2) Then he remembers how many fair opportunities of yielding to God he has basely lost; his spirit is like to faint when he remembereth that, as is said in another case – 'When I remember these things, I pour out my soul in me. O my God, my soul is cast down within me.

Deep calleth unto deep, all thy waves are gone over me.' [*Ps* 42:1–7.] (3) He now thinks of many Christians whom he mocked and despised in his heart, persuading himself now that they are happy, as having chosen the better part; he thinks of the condition of those who wait on Christ, as the queen of Sheba did of Solomon's servants: 'Happy are thy servants,' saith she, 'who stand continually before thee, and that hear thy wisdom. [1 *Kings* 10:8.] 'Blessed are they that dwell in Thy house.' [*Ps* 84:4.] He wishes to be one of the meanest who have any relation to God; as the *prodigal son* speaks, he would be as 'one of his father's hired servants.' [*Luke* 15:17, 19.] (4) Then he calls to mind the good report that is going abroad of God, according to that testimony of the prophet, who knew that God was a 'gracious God, and merciful, slow to anger, and of great kindness.' [*Jonah* 4:2.] The free and large promises and offers of grace come in here; and the gracious dealings of God with sinners of all sorts, as recorded in Scripture. (5) He thinks with himself, 'Why hath God spared me so long? and why have I got such a sight of my sin? and why hath He kept me from breaking prison at my own hand? why hath He made this strange change in me? It may be it is in His heart to do me good; O that it may be so!' Although all these thoughts be not in the preparatory work of every one, yet they are with many, and very promising where they are.

7. Upon all these thoughts and meditations the man, more seriously than ever before, resolveth to pray, and to make some attempt with God, upon life and death; he concludes, 'It can be no worse with him; for if he sit still he perisheth'; as the lepers speak. [2 *Kings* 7:3, 4.] He considers, with the perishing prodigal son, 'that there is bread enough in his father's house and to spare, whilst he

perisheth for want'; so he goes to God, for he knows not what else to make of his condition, as the prodigal son doth. And it may be, here he resolves what to speak; but things soon vary when he is present before God, as the prodigal son forgot some of his premeditated prayers. 'I will arise, and go to my Father, and will say unto him, Father, I have sinned against Heaven and before thee, and am no more worthy to be called thy son; make me as one of thy hired servants. And he arose and came unto his father, and said unto him, Father, I have sinned against Heaven, and in thy sight, and am no more worthy to be called thy son.' [*Luke* 15:17–21.]

And now, when he cometh before God, more observable than ever before – (1) He beginneth, with the publican, *afar off*, with many thorough confessions and self-condemnings, in which he is very liberal, as [*Luke* 15:21] – 'I have sinned against Heaven and before thee, and am no more worthy,' etc. (2) Now his thoughts are occupied as to the hearing of his prayers, which he was not wont to question much: he now knows what those expressions of the saints concerning the hearing of their prayers do import. (3) It is observable in this address, that there are many broken sentences, like that of *Ps* 6:3 – 'But Thou, O Lord, how long?' supplied with sighs and 'groanings which cannot be uttered,' and anxiously looking upward, thereby speaking more than can be well expressed by words. (4) There are ordinarily some interruptions, and, as it were, diversions; the man speaking sometimes to the enemy, sometimes to his own heart, sometimes to the multitudes in the world, as David doth in other cases – 'O thou enemy, destructions are come to a perpetual end.' [*Ps* 9:6.] 'Why art thou cast down, O my soul? and why art thou disquieted in me? hope thou in God, for I shall yet praise Him, who is the help of my countenance.' [*Ps* 42:6.] 'O ye sons of men, how long will ye turn my glory into shame?' [*Ps* 4:2.] (5) It is observable here that sometimes the man will halt, and be silent, to hear some indistinct whisperings of a joyful sound glancing on the mind, or some news in some broken word of Scripture, which, it may be, the man scarcely knoweth to be Scripture, or whether it is come from God, or whether an insinuation from Satan to delude him; yet this he hath resolved, only to 'hear what God the Lord will speak,' as upon another occasion. [*Ps* 85:8.] (6) More distinct promises come into the man's mind, on which he attempts to lay hold, but is beaten off with objections, as in another case the Psalmist is – 'But thou art holy – But I am a worm.' [*Ps* 22:3, 6.] Now it is about the dawning of the day with the man, and faith will stir as soon as the Lord imparteth 'the joyful sound.' [*Ps* 89:15.] This is the substance of the covenant, which may be shortly summed up in these words, 'Christ Jesus is my beloved Son, in whom I am well pleased; hear ye him.' [*Matt* 17:5.]

We can speak no further of the man's exercise as a preparatory work; for what followeth is more than preparatory; yet that the exercise may appear complete and full, we shall add here, that after all these things, the Lord, it may be, after many answers of divers sorts, mightily conveyeth the knowledge of His covenant into the heart, and determines the heart to close with it; and God now draweth his soul so to Christ [*John* 6:44], and so layeth out the heart for Him, that the work cannot miscarry; for now the heart is so enlarged for Him, as that less cannot satisfy, and more is not desired; like that of *Ps* 73:25 – 'Whom have I in heaven but Thee? or whom have I desired on earth beside Thee? The soul now resolves to die if He shall so command, yet at His door, and looking towards Him.

We have stated this preparatory work at some length, not tying any man to such particular circumstances: only we say, the Lord dealeth so with some; and where He so convinceth of sin, corruption, and self-emptiness, and makes a man take salvation to heart as the one thing necessary, and sets him to work in the use of the means which God hath appointed for relief; I say, such a work rarely shall be found to fail of a good issue and gracious result.

SECTION III

The difference between that preparatory work of the law which leads to salvation and the temporary convictions of those who relapse

1 *Objection:* Hypocrites and reprobates have great stirrings of conscience, and deep convictions about sin, setting them to work sometimes; and I do suspect any preparatory work of the law I ever had, to be but such as they have.

Answer: It will be hard to give sure essential differences between the preparatory work in those in whom afterwards Christ is formed, and those legal stirrings which are sometimes in reprobates. If there were not some gracious result of these convictions and awakenings of conscience in the Lord's people, and other marks, of which we shall speak afterwards, it were hard to adventure upon any difference that is clear in these legal stirrings. Yet, for answer to the objection, I shall offer some things, which rarely will be found in the stirrings of reprobates, and which are ordinarily found in that law-work which hath a gracious issue.

1. The convictions of hypocrites and reprobates are usually confined to some few very gross transgressions. Saul grants no more but the *persecuting of David.* [1 *Sam* 26:21.] Judas grants only the *betraying of innocent blood* [*Matt* 27:4]; but usually those convictions by which the Lord prepareth His own way in the soul, although they may begin at one or more gross particular transgressions, yet they stop not; but the man is led on to see many breaches of the law, and 'innumerable evils compassing Him' [*Ps* 40:12], as David speaketh in the sight of his sin. And withal, that universal conviction, if I may call it so, is not general, as usually we hear senseless men saying, 'that in all things they sin'; but it is particular and condescending, as Paul afterwards spake of himself: he not only is the chief of sinners, but particularly, he was a blasphemer a persecutor. [1 *Tim* 1:13.]

2. The convictions which hypocrites have, do seldom reach their corruption, and that body of death which works an aversion to what is good, and strongly inclines to what is evil. Ordinarily where we find hypocrites speaking of themselves in Scripture, they speak loftily, and with some self-conceit, as to their freedom from corruption. The Pharisees say to the poor man, 'Thou wast altogether born in sin, and dost thou teach us?' [*John* 9:34]; as if they themselves were not as corrupt by nature as he. They speak of great sins, as Hazael did – 'Am I a dog, that I should do this great thing?' [2 *Kings* 8:13]; and also in their undertakings of duty, as that *scribe* spake, 'Master, I will follow Thee whithersoever Thou goest.' [*Matt* 8:19.] See how the people speak: 'Then they said to Jeremiah, The Lord be a true and

faithful witness between us, if we do not even according to all things for the which the Lord thy God shall send thee to us. Whether it be good, or whether it be evil, we will obey the voice of the Lord our God, to whom we send thee; that it may be well with us when we obey the voice of the Lord our God.' [*Jer* 42:5, 6.] They undertake to do all that God will command them: so that they still 'go about,' in any case, 'to establish their own righteousness, not submitting unto the righteousness of God.' [*Rom* 10:3.] But I may say, that convictions and exercise about corruption, and that body of death, inclining them to evil, and disabling for good, is not the least part of the work where the Lord is preparing His own way. They judge themselves very wretched because of the body of sin, and are at their wits' end how to be delivered, as Paul speaks when he is under the exercise of it afterwards – 'O wretched man that I am, who shall deliver me from the body of this death.' [*Rom* 7:24.]

3. It will generally be found, that the convictions which are in hypocrites either are not so serious, as that some other business will not put them out of mind before any satisfaction is gotten; as in Cain, who went and built a city, and we hear no more of his conviction [*Gen* 4]; Felix went away until a more convenient time, and we hear no more of his trembling [*Acts* 24:25]; or, if that work becomes very serious, then it runneth to the other extremity, even despair of relief, leaving no room for escape. So we find Judas very serious in his convictions, yet he grew desperate, and hanged himself. [*Matt* 27:4, 5.] But where the Lord prepares His own way, the work is both so serious, that the person cannot be put off it, until he find some satisfaction, and yet under that very seriousness he lies open for relief; both which are clear from the

jailer's words, 'What must I do to be saved?' [*Acts* 16:30.] This serious inquiry after relief is a very observable thing in the preparatory work which leadeth on to Christ. Yet we desire none to lay too much weight on these things, since God has allowed clear differences between the precious and the vile.

2 *Objection:* I still fear I have not had so thorough a sight of my sin and misery as the Lord giveth to many whom He effectually calleth, especially to great transgressors such as I am.

Answer: It is true, the Lord discovereth to some clear views of their sin and misery, and they are thereby put under great legal terrors; but as all are not brought in by that sensible preparatory work of the law, as we showed before, so even those who are dealt with after that way are very differently and variously exercised in regard of the degrees of terror, and of the continuance of that work. The jailer had a violent work of very short continuance; Paul had a work continuing three days; some persons are 'in bondage through fear of death all their lives.' [*Heb* 2:15.] So that we must not limit the Lord to one way of working here. The main thing we are to look unto in these legal awakenings and convictions of sin and misery is, if the Lord reach those ends in us for which usually these stirrings and convictions are sent into the soul; and if those ends be reached, it is well; we are not to vex ourselves about any preparatory work further. Now, those ends which God seeks to accomplish with sinners by these legal terrors and awakenings of conscience are four.

First, The Lord discovers a sight of men's sin and misery to them, to chase them out of themselves, and to put them out of conceit of their own righteousness. Men naturally have high thoughts of themselves, and incline much to the covenant of works; the Lord therefore discovers to them so much of their sin and corruption, even in their best things, that they are made to loathe themselves, and despair of relief in themselves; and so they are forced to flee out of themselves, and from the covenant of works, to seek refuge elsewhere. [*Heb* 6:18.] 'They become dead to themselves, and the law,' as to the point of justification. [*Rom* 7:4.] Then 'have they no more confidence in the flesh.' [*Phil* 3:3.] This is supposed in the offers of Christ 'coming to seek and save that which is lost' [*Luke* 19:10]; and 'to be a physician to those who are sick.' [*Matt* 9:12.]

The *second* great end is, to commend Christ Jesus to men's hearts above all things, that so they may fall in love with Him, and betake themselves to that treasure and jewel which only enricheth [*Matt* 13:44]; and by so doing may serve the Lord's design in the contrivance of the gospel, which was the manifestation of His free grace through Christ Jesus in the salvation of men. The sight of a man's own misery and lost estate by nature is a ready way to make him prize Christ highly, who alone can set such a wretch at liberty; yea, it not only leadeth a man to a high esteem of Christ, but also of all things that relate to that way of salvation, as grace, the new covenant, faith, etc., and maketh him carefully gather and treasure up his *Michtams*, or golden scriptures, for the confirmation of his interest in these things.

The *third* great end is, to deter and frighten people from sin, and make them quarrel with it, and consent to put their neck under Christ's yoke. God kindles some sparks of hell in men's bosoms by the discovery of their sin, as a ready means to make them henceforth stand in awe, knowing 'how bitter a thing it is to depart from the Lord.'

[*Jer* 2:19.] So we find rest offered to the weary, upon condition they will take Christ's yoke: 'Take my yoke upon you, and learn of me, for I am meek and lowly in heart: and ye shall find rest unto your souls.' [*Matt* 11:29.] And God offereth to own men as their God and Father, upon condition they will allow no peaceable abode to Belial: 'What fellowship hath righteousness with unrighteousness? and what communion hath light with darkness? and what concord hath Christ with Belial? or what part hath he that believeth with an infidel? Wherefore come out from among them, and be ye separate, saith the Lord, and touch not the unclean thing, and I will receive you, and will be a Father unto you, and ye shall be my sons and daughters, saith the Lord Almighty.' [2 *Cor* 6:14–18.]

The *fourth* great end is, to work in men a patient and thankful submission to all the Master's pleasure. This is a singular piece of work: 'Then shalt thou remember, and be confounded, and never open thy mouth any more, because of thy shame, when I am pacified towards thee, for all that thou hast done, saith the Lord.' [*Ezek* 16:63.] The sight of a man's own vileness and deservings makes him silent, and constrains him to lay his hand on his mouth, whatsoever God doth unto him: 'I was dumb and opened not my mouth, because Thou didst it.' [*Ps* 39:9.] 'God hath punished us less than our iniquities.' [*Ezra* 9:13.] 'I will bear the indignation of the Lord, because I have sinned.' [*Mic* 7:9.] The man careth not what God doth to him, or how He deal with him, if only He save him from the deserved wrath to come: also any mercy is great mercy to him who hath seen such a sight of himself; 'he is less than the least of mercies.' [*Gen* 32:10.] 'Any crumb falling from the Master's table' is welcome. [*Matt*

15:27.] He thinks it 'rich mercy that he is not consumed.' [*Lam* 3:22.] This is the thing that marvellously maketh God's poor afflicted people so silent under and satisfied with their lot; nay, they think he deserveth hell who openeth his mouth at anything God doth to him, since he hath pardoned his transgressions.

So then, for satisfying the objection, I say, if the Lord have driven thee out of thyself, and commended Christ to thy heart above all things, and made thee resolve, in His strength, to wage war with every known transgression, and thou art in some measure as a weaned child, acquiescing in what He doth unto thee, desiring to lay thy hand on thy mouth thankfully; then thy convictions of sin and misery, and whatsoever thou dost plead as a preparatory work, is sufficient, and thou art to debate no more concerning it. Only be advised so to study new discoveries of the sense of thy lost condition every day, because of thy old and new sins; and also to seek fresh help in Christ, who is a priest for ever to make intercession; and to have the work of sanctification and patience with thankfulness renewed and quickened often: for somewhat of that work, which abaseth thee, exalteth Christ, and renders thee conformed to His will, must accompany thee throughout all thy life-time in this world.

CHAPTER III

Of faith as an evidence of an interest in Christ

We come now to speak of some more clear and sure marks by which men may discover their gracious state and interest in Christ. The *first* thing whereby men may know it, is their closing with Christ in the gospel wherein He is held forth. This is believing, or faith, which is the condition of the covenant: 'It is of faith, that it might be by grace.' [*Rom* 4:16.] Believe on the Lord Jesus Christ, and thou shalt be saved.' [*Acts* 16:31.] Now, although, in propriety of speech, it is hard to prove an interest by faith, it being our very interest in Him; yet the heart's closing with Christ Jesus is so discernible in itself, that we may well place it amongst the marks of a gracious state: and if a man can make out this, that he believeth on and in Christ Jesus, he thereby proves a very true interest in Him.

1 MISTAKES AS TO WHAT FAITH IS

Many scare at this as a mark, upon one of these three grounds:

1. Some conceive faith to be a difficult, mysterious thing, hardly attainable. To these I say, Do not mistake: faith is not so difficult as many apprehend it to be. I grant true faith in the lowest degree is the gift of God, and above the power of flesh and blood; for God must draw men to Christ. 'No man can come to me, except the

Father which hath sent me draw him.' [*John* 6:44.] 'Unto you it is given in the behalf of Christ to believe on Him.' [*Phil* 1:29.] Yet it were a reflection upon Christ, and all He hath done, to say it were a matter of insuperable difficulty; as is clear: 'The righteousness which is of faith speaketh on this wise, Say not in thine heart, Who shall ascend into heaven? that is, to bring Christ down from above; or, Who shall descend into the deep? that is, to bring up Christ again from the dead. But what saith it? The word is nigh thee, even in thy mouth, and in thy heart; that is, the word of faith which we preach, That if thou shalt confess with thy mouth the Lord Jesus, and shalt believe in thine heart that God hath raised Him from the dead, thou shalt be saved: for with the heart man believeth unto righteousness, and with the mouth confession is made unto salvation. For the Scripture saith, Whosoever believeth on Him shall not be ashamed.' [*Rom* 10:6–11.] It were, according to that scripture, as much upon the matter as to say, Christ came not from heaven, is not risen from the dead, nor ascended victorious to heaven. I say, He hath made the way to heaven most easy; and faith, which is the condition required on our part, more easy than men do imagine. For the better understanding of this, consider that justifying faith is not to believe that I am elected, or to believe that God loveth me, or that Christ died for me, or the like: these things are indeed very difficult, and almost impossible to be attained at the first by those who are serious; whilst natural atheists and deluded hypocrites find no difficulty in asserting all those things: I say, true justifying faith is not any of the aforesaid things; neither is it simply the believing of any sentence that is written, or that can be thought upon. I grant, he that believeth on Christ Jesus believeth what God hath said concerning man's sinful, miserable conditon by nature; and he believeth that to be true, that 'there is life in the Son, who was slain, and is risen again from the dead,' etc.: but none of these, nor the believing of many such truths, evinces justifying faith, or that believing on the Son of God spoken of in Scripture; for then it were simply an act of the understanding; but true justifying faith, which we now seek after, as a good mark of an interest in Christ, is chiefly and principally an act or work of the heart and will; having presupposed sundry things about truth in the understanding – 'With the heart man believeth unto righteousness.' [*Rom* 10:10.] And although it seem (verse 9), that a man is saved upon condition that he believes this truth, namely, that 'God raised Christ from the dead,' yet we must understand another thing there, and verse 10, than the believing the truth of that proposition; for besides that all devils have that faith, whereby they believe that God raised Christ from the dead; so the Scripture hath clearly resolved justifying faith into a *receiving* of Christ: 'As many as received Him, to them gave He power to become the sons of God, even to them that believe on His name.' [*John* 1:12.] The *receiving* of Christ is there explained to be the *believing on His name*. It is also called a *staying on the Lord* [*Is* 26:3]; a *trusting in God*, often mentioned in the Psalms, and the word is *a leaning on Him*. It is a *believing on Christ:* 'This is the work of God, that ye believe on Him whom He hath sent' [*John* 6:29], and often so expressed in the New Testament. When God maketh men believe savingly, He is said to *draw* them unto Christ; and when the Lord inviteth them to believe, He calleth them to come to Him. 'All that the Father giveth me, shall come to me; and him that cometh to me, I will in no wise cast out. No man can come to me, except the Father which hath sent me draw him.' [*John* 6:37, 44.] The kingdom of heaven is like a man finding a jewel, with which he falleth in love: 'The kingdom of heaven is like unto a treasure hid in a field; the which when a man hath found, he hideth, and for joy thereof, goeth and selleth all that he hath, and buyeth that field. Again, the kingdom of heaven is like unto a merchant-man seeking goodly pearls; who, when he had found one pearl of great price, went and sold all that he had, and bought it.' [*Matt* 13:44–46.] Now, I say this acting of the heart on Christ Jesus is not so difficult a thing as is conceived. Shall that be judged a mysterious difficult thing which doth consist much in desire? If men have but an appetite, they have it; for they are 'blessed that hunger after righteousness.' [*Matt* 5:6.] 'If you will,' you are welcome. [*Rev* 22:17.] Is it a matter of such intricacy and insuperable difficulty, earnestly *to look* to that exalted Saviour: 'Look unto me and be ye saved, all the ends of the earth.' [*Is* 45:22.] And to receive a thing that is offered, held forth, and declared to be mine, if I will but accept and take it, and in a manner 'open my mouth,' and give way to it?' 'Open thy mouth wide and I will fill it.' [*Ps* 81:10.] Such a thing is faith, if not less. Oh, if I could persuade people what justifying faith is, which appropriateth Christ to me! We often drive people from their just rest and quiet, by making them apprehend faith to be some deep, mysterious thing, and by exciting unnecessary doubts about it, whereby it is needlessly darkened.

2. Some make no use of this mark, as judging it a high presumptuous crime to pretend to so excellent a thing as is the very condition of the new covenant. To these I say, you need not startle so much at it, as if it were high pride to pretend to it; for whatsoever true faith be, men must

resolve to have it, or nothing at all: all other marks are in vain without it: a thousand things besides will not do the business: unless a man believe, he abideth in the state of condemnation. 'He that believeth not is condemned already because he hath not believed in the name of the only begotten Son of God. He that believeth not the Son shall not see life, but the wrath of God abideth on him.' [*John* 3:18, 36.]

3. Others do not meddle with this noble mark of faith, because they judge it a work of the greatest difficulty to find out where faith is. To these I say, it is not so difficult to find it out, since 'he that believeth, hath the witness in himself.' [1 *John* 5:10.] It is a thing which by some serious search may be known. Not only may we do much to find it out by the preparatory work going before it in many, as the apprehending and believing of a man's lost estate, and that he cannot work out his own salvation, and that there is a satisfying fulness in Christ, very desirable if he could obtain it; a serious minding of this, with a heart laid open for relief; as also by the ordinary companions and concomitants of it, namely, the liking of Christ's dominion, His kingly and prophetical office, a desire to resign myself wholly up to Him, to be at His disposing; as also by the native consequences of it, namely, the acquitting of the Word, the acquitting of my own conscience according to the Word, a heart-purifying work, a working by love, etc.; I say, not only may we know faith by these things, but it is discernible by itself and of its own nature. Although I deny not but there must be some help of God's Spirit, 'by which we know what is freely given unto us of God' [1 *Cor* 2:12]; as also, that God hath allowed many evidences and marks as precious helps, whereby men may clear up faith more fully to themselves – 'These

things have I written unto you that believe on the name of the Son of God, that ye may know that ye have eternal life' [1 *John* 5:13]; yet I still say that faith, or believing, which is some acting of the heart upon Christ in the gospel, and the transacting with Him there, is discernible of itself, and by itself, to a judicious understanding person, with an ordinary influence of the Spirit: unless the Lord, for reasons known to Himself, overcloud a man's reflex light, by which he should perceive what is in him.

2 TRUE SAVING FAITH DESCRIBED

This justifying faith, which we assert to be so discernible, is, in the Lord's deep wisdom and gracious condescension, variously expressed in Scripture, according to the different actings of it upon God, and outgoings after Him; so that every one who hath it may find and take it up in his own mould. It sometimes acts by a desire of union with Him in Christ; this is that *looking* to Him in Isaiah – 'Look unto Me and be ye saved, all the ends of the earth.' [*Is* 45:22.] This seems to be a weak act of faith, and far below other actings of it at other times perhaps in that same person. Men will look to what they dare not approach (in their apprehension), which they dare not touch or embrace; they may look to one to whom they dare not speak: yet God hath made the promise to faith in that acting, as the fore-cited scripture shows: and this He hath done mercifully and wisely; for this is the only discernible way of the acting of faith in some. Such are the actings or outgoings of faith expressed in Scripture by 'hungering and thirsting after righteousness' [*Matt* 5:6], and that expressed by *willing* – 'And whosoever will, let him take the water of life freely.' [*Rev* 22:17.]

Again, this faith goeth out sometimes in the act of recumbency, or leaning on the Lord, the soul taking up Christ then as a resting-stone, and God hath so held Him out, although He be a stumbling-stone to others. [*Rom* 9:33.] This acting of it is hinted in the expressions of *trusting* and *staying* on God, so often mentioned in Scripture; and precious promises are made to this acting of faith – 'God will keep them in perfect peace whose minds are stayed on Him; because such do trust in Him. Trust in the Lord: for with Him is everlasting strength.' [*Is* 26:3, 4.] 'They that trust in the Lord shall be as Mount Zion, which abideth for ever.' [*Ps* 125:1.] I say, the Lord hath made promises to this way of faith's acting, as knowing it will often go out after Him in this way with many persons; and this way of its acting will be most discernible to them.

It goeth out after God sometimes by an act of waiting. When the soul hath somewhat depending before God, and hath not clearly discovered his mind concerning it, then faith doth wait; and so it hath the promise – 'They shall not be ashamed that wait for me.' [*Is* 49:23.] Sometimes it acteth in a wilful way upon the Lord, when the soul apprehendeth God thrusting it away, and threatening its ruin – 'Though He slay me, yet will I trust in Him.' [*Job* 13:15.] The faith of that poor woman of Canaan [*Matt* 15], so highly commended by Christ, went out in this way of wilful acting over difficulties: and the Lord speaketh much good of it, and to it, because some will be at times called upon to exercise faith in that way, and so they have that for their encouragement. It were tedious to instance all the several ways of the acting of faith upon, and its exercise about, and outgoings after Christ – I may say, according to the various conditions of man. And accordingly faith, which God has appointed to traffic and travel between Christ and man, as the instrument of conveyance of His fulness unto man, and of maintaining union and communion with Him, acteth variously and differently upon God in Christ: for faith is the very shaping out of a man's heart according to God's device of salvation by Christ Jesus, 'in whom it pleased the Father that all fulness should dwell' [*Col* 1:19]; so that, let Christ turn what way He will, faith turneth and pointeth that way. Now He turns all ways in which He can be useful to poor man; and therefore faith acts accordingly on Him for drawing out of that fulness, according to a man's case and condition. As for example, The soul is *naked*, destitute of a covering to keep it from the storm of God's wrath; Christ is *fine raiment* [*Rev* 3:17, 18]; then accordingly faith's work here is to 'put on the Lord Jesus.' [*Rom* 13:14.] The soul is hungry and thirsty after somewhat that may everlastingly satisfy; Christ Jesus is 'milk, wine, water, the bread of life, and the true manna.' [*Is* 55:1, 2; *John* 6:48, 51.] He is 'the feast of fat things, and of wines on the lees well refined' [*Is* 25:6]: then the work and exercise of faith is to 'go, buy, eat, and drink abundantly.' [*John* 6:53, 57; *Is* 55:1.] The soul is pursued for guilt more or less, and is not able to withstand the charge: Christ Jesus is the city of refuge, and the high-priest there, during whose priesthood, that is, for ever, the poor man who escapes thither is safe; then the work and exercise of faith is 'to flee thither for refuge, to lay hold on the hope set before us.' [*Heb* 6:18.] In a word, whatsoever way He may benefit poor man, He declares Himself able to do. And as He holdeth out Himself in the Scriptures, so faith doth point towards Him. If He be a Bridegroom, faith will go out in a marriage relation; if He be a Father, faith pleadeth the man to be a child; if He be a Shepherd, faith pleads the man may be one of His sheep; if He be a Lord, faith calleth Him so, which none can do but by the Spirit of Jesus; if He be dead, and risen again for our justification, faith 'believeth God hath raised Him' on that account. [*Rom* 10:9.] Wheresoever He be, there would faith be; and whatsoever He is, faith would be somewhat like Him; for by faith the heart is laid out in breadth and length for Him; yea, when the fame and report of Him goeth abroad in His truth, although faith seeth not much, yet it 'believeth on His name,' upon the very fame He hath sent abroad of Himself. [*John* 1:12.]

2 FURTHER EXPLANATIONS CONCERNING SAVING FAITH

But here, for avoiding mistakes, consider –

1. That although justifying faith acts so variously, yet every believer who hath a good title to Christ Jesus hath not all these various actings and exercises of faith; for his condition requires them not; and also the Master is sometimes pleased not to lead out the faith of some persons, in all these particular ways, for reasons known to Himself, even when their necessity (to their apprehension) calleth for such an acting of faith. Surely, every one dare not say, 'Though He slay me, yet will I trust in Him.' [*Job* 13:15.] Many would not have gone up with the woman of Canaan, spoken of in *Matt* 15, but would have been discouraged, and have given up the pursuit. It is on this account that Christ highly commends the faith of some beyond the faith of others; as of the centurion, and the woman of Canaan. [*Matt* 8:10.] Many good people are much disquieted about their faith, because it goeth not

out in all those ways we find recorded in Scripture; but there is hardly any one to be found whose faith has acted all these ways.

2. Many of these actings of faith are much intended and remitted. They are sometimes strong and vigorous, and discernible; and sometimes they fail, and unbelief prevails, so it were an uncertain thing to judge of a man's state by these. We find the saints at times very different from themselves in regard of the actings of faith, as we showed before.

3. Each one of these actings of faith speaks good to the person in whom it is, and has promises annexed unto it, as we have said. Yet –

4. Although these actings of faith have promises annexed to them, they are not, on that account, the condition of the new covenant; for then every one behoved to have each one of them, which is not true, as we said before. A promise is made to him who overcometh: but perseverance is not the condition of the new covenant, though it supposeth it. There are promises made to the exercise of all graces in Scripture; but faith only is the condition of the covenant. I say, then, these promises are made to these workings of faith, not as such, but as they imply justifying faith, which is the condition of the covenant. All these are actings of faith, but not as it is justifying. Therefore –

5. There is something common to all gracious persons, which may be supposed by all the aforesaid actings of faith, wherein the nature and essence of justifying faith consist: and this is the heart's satisfaction with God's plan of salvation by Christ. When man is pleased with God's method of satisfaction to justice, through Christ Jesus, in whom all fulness now dwells, by the Father's pleasure; when the soul and heart of man acquiesce in that, then it

believeth unto salvation. As at first the Lord made man suitable to the covenant of works, by creating him perfect, and so putting him in a capacity to perform his will in that covenant: so, under the new covenant, when God giveth the new heart to man, He puts the idea and stamp of all His device in the new covenant upon the man, so as there is a consonance to God's will there: thus he bears the image of the second Adam, Christ Jesus, on him. This is a great part of the new heart, and is most opposed to works: since now the man absolutely falls from works, 'becoming dead to the law,' as to the point of justification, 'by the body of Christ.' [*Rom* 7:4.] Man perceiving that God hath devised a way of satisfying Divine justice, and recovering lost man by the incarnation of Christ, he thinks this so good and sure a way, that he absolutely gives up with the law, as I said before, and closes with this device; and this is believing or faith, very opposite to works, and all resting thereupon. This cannot fail to be in all gracious persons, in whom many of the actings of faith are not to be found. This doth clearly suppose known distress in a man, without any relief in himself: this supposes known fulness in Christ, as the alone sufficient relief: this imports a sort of appropriation; for the heart, being pleased with that device, in so far swayeth towards it. This is a thing clearly supposed in all the actings of faith spoken of before. He that greedily hungereth, hath this; and he that leaneth hath this, etc. This is to esteem 'Christ the wisdom and power of God' to salvation, as He is said to be to all that believe. [1 *Cor* 1:24.] They esteem that device wise and sure, becoming God; and that is to believe. On this account, Christ, who is the stone rejected by many, is 'precious to them who believe'; a fit stone to recover, fortify, and beautify the tottering building and fabric of lost man – 'To whom coming, as unto a living stone, disallowed indeed of men, but chosen of God and precious; ye also, as lively stones, are built up a spiritual house, a holy priesthood, to offer up spiritual sacrifices, acceptable to God by Jesus Christ. Wherefore it is also contained in the Scripture, Behold, I lay in Zion a chief corner-stone, elect, precious; and he that believeth on Him shall not be confounded. Unto you, therefore, which believe He is precious; but unto them which be disobedient, the stone which the builders disallowed, the same is made the head of the corner; and a stone of stumbling, and a rock of offence, even to them which stumble at the word, being disobedient, whereunto also they were appointed.' [1 *Peter* 2:4–8.] 'The kingdom of God is like a man finding a treasure, for which with joy he selleth all.' [*Matt* 13:44.] These words hold out the very way of believing, namely, salvation is discovered in the gospel to be by Christ; the heart valueth that method as satisfying. This is to believe on the Son of God lifted up; which is compared with looking to the brazen serpent. [*John* 3:14.] It was man's approbation of that device which made it effectual for his healing; so is it here, 'He that so believeth, setteth to his seal that God is true.' [*John* 3:33.] True! Wherein? In that record He hath borne, that God hath provided life for men, and placed it all in Christ. 'He that believeth not maketh God a liar.' [1 *John* 5:10.] Wherein? In His saying that Christ is a safe and sure way to heaven. This is being pleased with and acquiescing in that device; and it is consonant to all I know spoken of justifying faith in Scripture. This is the believing on Christ and on His name, the receiving of Him, and resting on Him for salvation, in our Catechism; the believing that Jesus is the Christ, that is, the anointed One, whom the

Father hath sealed and set apart, and qualified for the work of reconciling man unto God; and 'he that believeth that Jesus is the Christ, is born of God.' [1 *John* 5:1.] This is to 'believe with the heart that God hath raised Christ from the dead.' [*Acts* 8:37.] The man believeth Christ died and rose on the account of satisfaction for man's transgression. Devils may believe that: nay, but the man I speak of, 'believeth it with the heart' (which no natural man doth, until a new heart be given unto him); that is, he is cordially pleased, and satisfied with and acquiesceth in, this glorious method. And thus faith layeth out itself now and then in its actings, out-goings, and exercise, according to all the covenant relations under which Christ is held forth in the Scripture.

Now, I say, this faith is discernible, not only in these actings – many times a man may know if his heart doth hunger after Christ, and flee for refuge to Him when pursued, and if he doth commit himself unto God, etc. – but also in its very nature; as it is justifying, it is discernible, and may be known. A man may clearly know, if from known distress in himself, upon the report and fame of Christ's fulness, his heart is pleased with God's device in the new covenant; if it goeth after Christ in that discovery and approveth Him as Lord of the life of men, terminating and resting there, and nowhere else, acquiescing in that contrivance with desire and complacency. This is a discernible thing; therefore I call upon men impartially to examine themselves, and if they find that their heart has closed so with that device of salvation, and is gone out after Him as precious, that thereupon they conclude a sure and true interest in Jesus Christ, and a good claim and title to the crown, since 'he that believeth shall never perish, but have everlasting life.' [*John* 3:16, 36.]

4 THE DIFFERENCE BETWEEN THE FAITH OF HYPOCRITES AND TRUE SAVING FAITH

Objection: Hypocrites and reprobates have a sort of faith, and are said to believe; and cannot choose but go out after Christ, and that device of salvation, when they hear of it; and they profess they do so, yet are deluded, and so may I. 'Many believed in His name, when they saw the miracles which he did. But Jesus did not commit Himself unto them, because He knew all men.' [*John* 2:23, 24.] 'Then Simon the sorcerer himself believed also.' [*Acts* 8:13.]

Answer: To say nothing of that thought of your heart, whereby you wonder that any man should not approve of the device of salvation by Christ, and be led out towards Him, as a very promising thing, and implying that justifying faith is in your bosom; and, to say nothing in contradiction to that which you think, that a natural man, whilst such, and before he gets a new heart, can be pleased with that device, and affectionately believe with his heart that which perfectly overthrows the covenant of works, and abaseth man in the point of self-righteousness already attained, or that can be attained by him, which is inconsistent with many scriptural truths; I shall notice the following differences between the faith of all hypocrites or reprobates, and that true saving justifying faith, whereof we have spoken.

1. They never close with Christ Jesus in that device, and Him alone, as a sufficient covering of the eyes, as is said of Abraham to Sarah [*Gen* 20:16]; they still hold fast somewhat of their own, at least to help to procure God's favour and salvation; their heart doth still speak, as that young man in Luke insinuates, 'What shall I do to inherit

eternal life?' [*Luke* 10:25; 18:18.] Besides that, they still retain their former lovers, and will not break their covenants with hell and death, imagining they may have Christ with these things equally sharing in their heart; contrary to that, 'A man cannot serve two masters.' [*Matt* 6:24.] Either Christ must be judged absolute Lord, and worthy to be so, or nothing at all; and so it is clear their heart is not prepared for that device of salvation by Christ, whom God hath alone made Lord here, in whom all fulness shall dwell. But where justifying faith is, the soul of a man and his heart doth close with Christ, and Him alone, 'having no confidence in the flesh,' and trusting only in God. [*Phil* 3:3; *Ps* 62:5.] Also the man here giveth up all other lovers; as they compete with Christ, he resolves 'not to be for another.' [*Hos* 3:3.] He calls Him Lord, which a man can only do by the Spirit of Christ.

2. As hypocrites and reprobates never close with Christ alone, so they never fully close with Christ as anointed to be a King, to rule over a man in all things; a Priest, to procure pardon and to make peace for man upon all occasions; a Prophet, to be wisdom, and a teacher and counsellor in all cases to man: so they do not receive Christ, especially in the first and third offices. But where true justifying faith is, a man closeth wholly with Christ in all His offices, judging all His will 'good, holy, just, and spiritual' [*Rom* 7:12]; and 'right concerning all things' [*Ps* 119:128]; 'making mention of His righteousness only.' [*Ps* 71:16.]

The man also giveth up himself to be taught of Him – 'Learn of me.' [*Matt* 11:29.] So that 'Christ is made,' to the true believer, with His own consent, 'wisdom, righteousness, sanctification, and redemption.' [1 *Cor*

1:30.] And although he has not all these things formally in exercise when his heart goeth out after Christ, yet, upon search and trial, it will be found with him as I have said.

3. Hypocrites and reprobates never close with Christ, and all the inconveniences that may follow Him; they stick at that, with the scribe – 'And a certain scribe came and said unto Him, Master, I will follow Thee whithersoever Thou goest. And Jesus saith unto him, The foxes have holes, and the birds of the air have nests; but the Son of Man hath not where to lay His head.' [*Matt* 8:19, 20.] But where true justifying faith is, a man closes with Him at all hazards; he resolves to forego all rather than forego Christ. 'We have left all and followed Thee' [*Mark* 10:28]; 'he reckoned all to be loss and dung for the excellency of Christ Jesus, as his Lord, and to be found in Him.' [*Phil* 3:8.]

We might point out other differences also, as that true faith is operative, 'purifying the heart' [*Acts* 15:9]; 'working by love' [*Gal* 5:6]; whilst hypocrites do only cleanse the 'outside of the platter' [*Matt* 23:25]; and 'do all to be seen of men' [*Matt* 23:5]; 'not seeking the honour that is of God only' [*John* 5:44], and so cannot believe. We might also show, that true faith is never alone in a man, but attended with other saving graces. But because these things will coincide with what follows, and as we are showing here that a man may determine his gracious state by his faith, and the actings thereof on Christ, we pass these things for the present.

CHAPTER IV

Of the new creature as an evidence of an interest in Christ

The *second* great mark of a gracious state, and true saving interest in Jesus Christ, is the new creature – 'If any man be in Christ, he is a new creature.' [2 *Cor* 5:17.] This new creation or renovation of man, is a very sensible[1] change; although not in those who are effectually called from the womb, or in their younger years; because those have had this new creature from that time in them, so that this change in after-periods of time is not so discernible as in those who have been regenerated and brought unto Christ after they were come to greater age, and so have more palpably been under the 'power of darkness,' before they were 'translated into the kingdom of Christ.' [*Col* 1:13.] But in all who do warrantably pretend to Christ, this new creature must be; although some do not know experimentally the contraries of every part of it as others do; because they have not been equally, in regard of practice, under the power of darkness. This new creature is called the 'new man.' [*Col.* 3:10], which points out the extent of it. It is not simply a new tongue or new hand, but a *new man*. There is a principle of new life and motion put in the man, which is the new heart; which new principle of life sendeth forth acts of life, or of 'conformity to the image' of Him who created it, so that the party is renewed in some measure every way. [*Col* 3:10.] This renovation

[1] Sensible = known and felt.

of the man who is in Christ may be reduced into these two great heads:

I THE WHOLE MAN MUST BE TO SOME EXTENT RENEWED

There is a renovation of the man's person, soul and body, in some measure.

1. His understanding is renewed, so that he judgeth 'Christ preached' in the gospel to be 'the wisdom and power of God,' a wise and strong device beseeming God. [1 *Cor* 1:23, 24.] He knoweth the things of God really and solidly, not to be *yea and nay*, and uncertain fancies; but all to be *yea and amen*, solid, certain, substantial things, having a desirable accomplishment in Christ, and resolving much in Him. 'The natural man receiveth not the things of the Spirit of God; for they are foolishness unto him; neither can he know them, because they are spiritually discerned: but he that is spiritual judgeth all things.' [1 *Cor* 2:14, 15.] 'As God is true, our word toward you was not yea and nay. For the Son of God, Jesus Christ, who was preached among you by us, even by me, and Silvanus, and Timotheus, was not yea and nay, but in Him was yea. For all the promises of God in Him are yea, and in Him amen, unto the glory of God by us.' [2 *Cor* 1:18–20.] Natural men, educated under gospel ordinances, although they have some notional knowledge of God, Christ, the promises, the motions of the Holy Spirit, etc., so that they may confer, preach, and dispute about these things; yet they look on them as common received maxims of Christianity from which to recede were a singularity and disgrace; but not as real, solid, substantial truths, so as to venture their souls and everlasting being on them. The

understanding is renewed also, to understand somewhat of God in the creatures, as bearing marks of His glorious attributes [*Ps* 19:1]; they see the heavens declaring His glory and power; and somewhat of God in providence, and the dispensations that fall out: His wondrous works declare that His name is near. [*Ps* 75:1.] The understanding also perceives the conditions and cases of the soul otherwise than it was wont to do; as we find the saints usually speaking in Scripture – 'O my soul, thou hast said unto the Lord, Thou art my Lord.' [*Ps* 16:2.] 'My soul said, Thy face will I seek.' [*Ps* 27:8.] 'Why art thou cast down, O my soul?' 'Return unto thy rest, O my soul.' [*Ps* 42:5; 116:7.]

2. The heart and affections are renewed. The heart is made a new heart, a heart of flesh, capable of impressions, having a copy of His law stamped on it, and the fear of God put into it, whereby the man's duty becomes in a manner native and kindly to the man – 'A new heart also will I give you, and a new spirit will I put within you; and I will take away the stony heart out of your flesh, and I will give you an heart of flesh. And I will put my Spirit within you, and cause you to walk in my statutes, and ye shall keep my judgments and do them.' [*Ezek* 36:26, 27.] It was before a *heart of stone*, void of the fear of God. The affections are now renewed: the love is renewed in a good measure; it goeth out after God, after His law, and after those who have God's image in them, 'I will love the Lord' [*Ps* 18:1] – after His law, 'O how love I thy law!' [*Ps* 119:97] – after those who have God's image in them, 'By this shall all men know that ye are my disciples, if ye have love one to another.' [*John* 13:35.] 'We know that we have passed from death unto life, because we love the brethren.' [1 *John* 3:14.] This love to God's people

is purely on the account that they are the children of God, and keep His statutes: it is with a 'pure heart fervently' [1 *Peter* 1:22]; and therefore it goeth towards all those whom the man knows or apprehends to be such. 'I am a companion of all them that fear thee, and of them that keep thy precepts' [*Ps* 119:63] – in all cases and conditions, even where there is nothing to beautify or commend but the image of God. And this love is so *fervent* many times, that it putteth itself out in all relations; so that a man seeks a godly wife, a godly master, a godly servant, a godly counsellor, in preference to all others – 'Mine eyes shall be upon the faithful of the land, that they may dwell with me: he that walketh in a perfect way, he shall serve me.' [*Ps* 101:6.] And 'it is not quenched by many waters.' [*Cant* 8:7.] Many imperfections and infirmities, differences in opinion, wrongs received, will not altogether quench love. Also it is communicative of good according to its measure, and as the case of the godly poor requires – 'Thou art my Lord, my goodness extendeth not to thee, but to the saints,' etc. [*Ps* 16:2.] 'But whoso hath this world's good, and seeth his brother have need, and shutteth up his bowels of compassion from him, how dwelleth the love of God in him? My little children, let us not love in word, neither in tongue, but in deed and in truth. And hereby we know that we are of the truth, and shall assure our hearts before Him.' [1 *John* 3:17–19.] The man's hatred is also renewed, and is now directed against sin. 'I hate vain thoughts' [*Ps* 119:113]; against God's enemies, as such, 'Do not I hate them that hate Thee?' [*Ps* 139:21, 22.] The joy or delight is renewed, for it runneth towards God, 'Whom have I in heaven but thee? and there is none upon earth that I desire besides thee [*Ps* 73:25] – towards His law and will, 'His delight is in the law of the Lord' [*Ps* 1:2] – and towards the godly and their fellowship, 'To the saints in whom is all my delight.' [*Ps* 16:3.] The sorrow is turned against sin which hath wronged Christ – 'Looking to Him whom they have pierced, they mourn.' [*Zech* 12:10.] The sorrow is godly there, and against what encroacheth upon God's honour – 'They are sorrowful for the solemn assembly, and the reproach of that is their burden.' [*Zeph* 3:18.] There is some renovation in all the affections, as in every other part of the soul, pointing now towards God.

3. The very outward members of the man are renewed, as the Scripture speaks – the tongue, the eye, the ear, the hand, and the foot, so that those members which once were abused as weapons of unrighteousness unto sin, are now improved as weapons of righteousness unto holiness. [*Rom* 6:19.]

2 HE MUST BE RENEWED, TO SOME EXTENT, IN ALL HIS WAYS

A man who is in Christ is renewed in some measure in all his ways – 'Behold all things are become new.' [2 *Cor* 5:17.] The man becometh new.

1. In the way of his interest. He was set upon *any good* before, though but apparent and at best but external. 'Many say, Who will show us any good?' [*Ps* 4:6]; but now his interest and business is, how to 'be found in Christ, in that day' [*Phil* 3:9]; or how to be obedient to Him, and 'walk before Him in the light of the living' [*Ps* 56:13]; which He would choose among all the mercies that fill this earth – 'The earth, O Lord, is full of Thy mercy, teach me Thy statutes.' [*Ps* 119:64.] The interest of Christ also becomes the man's interest, as appears in

the song of Hannah and of Mary. [1 *Sam* 2; *Luke* 1.] It is strange to see people newly converted, and having reached but the beginnings of knowledge, concern and interest themselves in the public matters of Christ's kingdom, so desirous to have Him riding prosperously and subduing the people under Him.

2. The man that is in Christ is renewed in the way of his worship. He was wont to 'serve God in the oldness of the letter' [*Rom* 7:6]; according to custom, answering the letter of the command in outward duty which one in whom the old man hath absolute dominion can do; but now he worshippeth God in newness of spirit, in a new way, wherein He is 'helped by the Spirit of God' [*Rom* 8:26], beyond the reach of flesh and blood. He 'serveth now the true and living God' [1 *Thess* 1:9]; 'in spirit and in truth.' [*John* 4:23.] Having spiritual apprehensions of God, and engaged in his very soul in that work, doing and saying truly and not feignedly when he worshippeth; still desiring to approach unto Him as a living God, who heareth and seeth Him, and can accept His service. [*Ps* 62:1, 2.] I grant he fails of this many times; yet I may say, such worship he intends, and sometimes overtakes, and does not much reckon that worship which is not so performed unto God; and the iniquity of his holy things is not the least part of His burden and exercise. To such a worship natural men are strangers, whilst they babble out their vain-glorious boastings, like the Pharisee – 'Lord, I thank Thee that I am not as other men' [*Luke* 18:11, 12]; or the Athenians, who worshipped an 'unknown God.' [*Acts* 17:23.]

3. The man that is in Christ is renewed in the way of his outward calling and employments in the world; he now resolves to be diligent in it, because God hath so

commanded – Not slothful in business; fervent in spirit; serving the Lord' [*Rom* 12:11]; and to regard God in it as the last end, doing it to 'His glory' [1 *Cor* 10:31]; and studying to keep some intercourse with God in the exercise of his outward employments, as Jacob on his dying bed – 'I have waited for Thy salvation, O Lord' [*Gen* 49:18]; and as Nehemiah did – 'Then the king said unto me, For what dost thou make request? So I prayed to the God of heaven' [*Neh* 2:4]; so that the man resolves to walk with God, and 'set Him always before him' [*Ps* 16:8]; wherein I deny not that he often faileth.

4. He becomes new in the way of his relations; he becomes a more dutiful husband, father, brother, master, servant, neighbour, etc. Herein doth he exercise himself to keep a conscience void of offence towards men as well as towards God, 'becoming all things to all men.' [*Acts* 24:16; 1 *Cor* 9:22.]

5. He becomes new in the way of lawful liberties. He studies to make use of meat, drink, sleep, recreations, apparel, with an eye to God, labouring not to come under the power of any lawful thing – 'All things are lawful unto me, but all things are not expedient; all things are lawful for me, but I will not be brought under the power of any' [1 *Cor* 6:12]; nor to give offence to others in the use of these things – 'For meat destroy not the work of God. All things indeed are pure; but it is evil for that man who eateth with offence. It is good neither to eat flesh, nor to drink wine, nor any thing whereby thy brother stumbleth, or is offended, or is made weak.' [*Rom* 14:20, 21.] 'Let every one of us please his neighbour for his good to edification' [*Rom* 15:2] – not using 'liberty as an occasion to the flesh.' [*Gal* 5:13.] Yea, he laboureth to use all these

things as a stranger on earth, so that his moderation may appear: 'Let your moderation be known unto all men.' [*Phil* 4:5.] And he regards God as the last end in these things, 'doing all to the glory of God'; so that we may say of that man, 'Old things are' much 'passed away, all things are' in some measure 'become new.' [2 *Cor* 5:17.] He that is so a new creature is undoubtedly in Christ.

This renovation of a man in all manner of conversation, and this being under the law to God in all things, is that 'holiness without which no man shall see the Lord.' [*Heb* 12:14.] Men may fancy things to themselves, but unless they study to approve themselves unto God in all well-pleasing, and attain some inward testimony of sincerity that way, they shall not assure their hearts before Him. The testimony of men's conscience is their rejoicing. [2 *Cor* 1:12.] 'By this we know that we know Him, if we keep His commandments.' [1 *John* 2:3.] 'And hereby we know that we are of the truth, and shall assure our hearts before Him. For if our heart condemn us, God is greater than our heart, and knoweth all things. Beloved, if our heart condemn us not, then have we confidence towards God.' [1 *John* 3:19–21.] No confidence if the heart condemn. This is the new creature, having a principle of new spiritual life infused by God into the heart, whereby it becometh new, and putteth forth acts of new life throughout the whole man, as we have said, so that he pointeth towards the whole law – (1) Towards those commands which forbid sin; so he resolves to contend against secret sins, 'not to lay a stumbling-block before the blind' [*Lev* 19:14] – little sins, which are judged so by many, the least things of the law – 'Whosoever shall break one of these least commandments, and shall teach men so, he shall be called the least in the kingdom of heaven' [*Matt* 5:19]; spiritual sins, filthiness of the spirit – 'Having therefore these promises, dearly beloved, let us cleanse ourselves from all filthiness of the flesh and spirit, perfecting holiness in the fear of God' [2 *Cor* 7:1]; sins of omission as well as of commission, since men are to be judged by these – 'Then shall He say unto them on the left hand, Depart from Me, ye cursed, into everlasting fire, prepared for the devil and his angels: for I was an hungered and ye gave me no meat, I was thirsty and ye gave me no drink.' [*Matt* 25:42, 44.] Yea, sins that are wrought into his natural humour and constitution, and thus are as a right eye or hand to him – 'If thy right eye offend thee, pluck it out, and cast it from thee.' [*Matt* 5:29.] This new principle of life, by the good hand of God, makes the man set himself against every known sin, so far as not to allow peaceful abode to any known darkness – 'What fellowship hath righteousness with unrighteousness? and what communion hath light with darkness?' [2 *Cor* 6:14.] (2) As also he pointeth towards those commands which relate to duty, and the quickening of grace in man. It maketh a man respect all God's known commands [*Ps* 119:6]; to 'live godly, righteously, and soberly' [*Tit* 2:12]; yea and to study a right and sincere way and manner of doing things, resolving not to give over this study of conformity to God's will whilst he liveth on earth, but still to 'press forward toward the mark for the prize of the high calling of God in Christ Jesus.' [*Phil* 3:13, 14.] This is true holiness, every way becoming all those who pretend to be heirs of that holy habitation, in the immediate company and fellowship of a holy God – 'We know that when He shall appear we shall be like Him.' [1 *John* 3:2.]

3 THE SUPPOSED UNATTAINABLENESS OF SUCH A RENEWAL

Some may think these things high attainments, and very hard to be got at. I grant it is true. But –

First, Remember that there is a very large allowance in the covenant promised to His people, which maketh things more easy. The Lord has engaged 'to take away the stony heart, to give a heart of flesh, a new heart, a heart to fear Him for ever'; He hath engaged to 'put His law in men's heart; to put His fear in their heart, to make them keep that law; to put His Spirit in them, to cause them to keep it.' He hath promised 'to satisfy the priests with fatness,' that the souls of 'the people may be satisfied with His goodness: and to keep and water them continually every moment.' [*Ezek* 36:26, 27; *Jer* 31:12, 13, 14, 33; 32:32, 36, 40; *Is* 27:3.] And if He must be 'inquired of to do all these things unto men,' He engageth to pour out the Spirit of grace and supplication on them, and so to teach them how to seek these things, and how to put Him to it, to do all for them. [*Zech* 12:10.]

Secondly, For the satisfaction of weaker Christians, I grant this new creature, as we have circumscribed and enlarged it, will not be found in all the degrees of it in every gracious person. But it is well if –

1. There be a new man. We cannot grant less – 'If any man be in Christ, he is a new creature'; and that is the new man which all must put on who are savingly taught of Christ – 'If so be that ye have heard Him, and have been taught by Him, as the truth is in Jesus: that ye put off concerning the former conversation the old man, which is corrupt according to the deceitful lusts, and be renewed in the spirit of your mind: and that ye put on the

new man, which after God is created in righteousness and true holiness.' [*Eph* 4:21-24.] There must be some renewing after the image of God in a man's soul and body; there must be somewhat of every part of the man pointing towards God. Although I grant every one cannot instruct this to others, neither discern it in himself, because many know not the distinct parts of the soul, nor the reformation competent to every part of the soul and body; yet it will be found there is some such thing in them, yea, they have a witness of it within them, if you make the thing plain and clear to them what it is.

2. There must be such a respect unto God's known commands, that a man do not allow peaceably any known iniquity to dwell in him; for 'what fellowship hath righteousness with unrighteousness? and what communion hath light with darkness?' He must not regard iniquity – 'Then shall I not be ashamed when I have respect unto all Thy commandments.' 'If I regard iniquity in my heart, the Lord will not hear me.' [2 *Cor* 6:14-16; *Ps* 119:6; 66:18.] I grant men may be ignorant of many commands and many sins, and may imagine, in some cases, that some sins are not hateful to God; but supposing that they are instructed in these things, there can be no agreement between righteousness and unrighteousness.

3. Men must point towards all the law of God in their honest resolutions; for this is nothing else than to give up the heart unto God, to put His law in it without exception, which is a part of the covenant we are to make with God – 'This is the covenant that I will make with the house of Israel – I will put My laws into their mind, and write them in their hearts.' [*Heb* 8:10.] I grant many know not how to have respect to God's law in all their ways; but if it be made manifest to them how that should

be done, they will point at it. And it is true, they will many times fail of their resolutions in their practice; yet when they have failed, they can say they did resolve otherwise; and will again honestly and without guile, resolve to do otherwise; and it will prove their affliction to have failed of their resolution, when the Lord discovers it to them, which He will do in due time.

4. When we are to judge of our state by the new creature, we must do it at a convenient time, when we are in good case; at least, not when we are in the worst case; for 'the flesh and spirit do lust and fight against each other' [*Gal* 5:17]; and sometimes the one, and sometimes the other doth prevail. Now, I say, we must choose a convenient time when the spiritual part is not by some temptation worsted and overpowered by the flesh; for in that case the new creature is driven back in its streams, and much returned to the fountain and the habits, except in some small things not easily discernible, whereby it maketh opposition to the flesh, according to the foresaid scripture. For now it is the time of winter in the soul, and we may not expect fruit; yea, not leaves, as in some other seasons. Only here, lest profane atheists should take advantage of this, we will say, that the spirit doth often prevail over the flesh in a godly man, and that the scope, aim, tenor, and main drift of his way is in the law of the Lord; that is his *walk* [*Ps* 119:1]; whereas the pathway and ordinary course of the wicked is sin, as is often hinted in the book of the Proverbs of Solomon. And if it happen that a godly man be overcome by any transgression, ordinarily it is his sad vexation: and we suppose he keeps it still in dependency before God to have it rectified, as David speaketh, 'Wilt thou not deliver my feet from falling?' [*Ps* 56:13.]

CHAPTER V

The difference between the true christian and the hypocrite

Objection: Atheists and hypocrites may have great changes and renovations wrought upon them, and in them, and I fear such may be the case with me.

Answer: I grant that atheists and hypocrites have many things in them which look like the new creature.

First, in regard of the parts of the man, they may (1) Come to much knowledge, as [*Heb* 6:4] 'They are enlightened.' (2) There may be an exciting of their affections, as 'They receive the word with joy,' as he that received the seed into stony places. [*Matt* 13:20.] (3) They may effect a great deal of reformation in the outward man, both as to freedom from sin, and engagement to positive duty, as the Pharisee did – 'God, I thank Thee that I am not as other men are, extortioners, unjust, adulterers, or even as this publican; I fast twice in the week, I give tithes of all that I possess.' [*Luke* 18:11, 12.] Yea (4) In regard of their practical understanding, they may judge some things of God to be excellent: the officers said that 'never man spake as Christ.' [*John* 7:46.]

Secondly, Hypocrites may have a great deal of profession. (1) They may talk of the law and gospel, and of the covenant: as the wicked do – 'What hast thou to do to declare my statutes, or that thou should'st take my covenant in thy mouth?' [*Ps* 50:16.] (2) They may confess sin openly to their own shame, as King Saul did – 'Then said Saul, I have sinned: return, my son David;

for I will no more do thee harm, because my soul was precious in thine eyes this day: behold, I have played the fool, and have erred exceedingly.' [1 *Sam* 26:21.] (3) They may humble themselves in sackcloth, with Ahab – 'And it came to pass, when Ahab heard these words, that he rent his clothes, and put sackcloth upon his flesh, and fasted, and lay in sackcloth, and went softly.' [1 *Kings* 21:27.] (4) They may inquire busily after duty, and come cheerfully to receive it – 'Yet they seek me daily, and delight to know my ways, as a nation that did righteousness, and forsook not the ordinance of their God; they ask of me the ordinances of justice, they take delight in approaching to God.' [*Is* 58:2.] (5) They may join with God's interest in a hard and difficult time, as Demas and other hypocrites, who afterwards fell away. (6) They may give much of their goods to God and to the saints, as Ananias, if not all their goods – 'Though I bestow all my goods to feed the poor, and have not charity, it profiteth me nothing.' [*Acts* 5:1, 2; 1 *Cor* 13:3.] Yea (7) It is not impossible for some such, being straitly engaged in their credit, to 'give their bodies to be burned,' as in the last cited place.

Thirdly, Hypocrites may advance far in the common and ordinary steps of a Christian work; such as the elect have when God leads them captive. As (1) They may be under great convictions of sin, as Judas was – 'Then Judas, which had betrayed Him, when he saw that He was condemned, repented himself, and brought again the thirty pieces of silver to the chief priests and elders saying, I have sinned in that I have betrayed the innocent blood. And they said, What is that to us? see thou to that. And he cast down the pieces of silver in the temple, and departed, and went and hanged himself.' [*Matt* 27:3–5.]

So was King Saul often. (2) They may tremble at the word of God, and be under much terror, as Felix was – 'And as he reasoned of righteousness, temperance, and judgment to come, Felix trembled, and answered, Go thy way for this time, when I have a convenient season I will call for thee.' [*Acts* 24:25.] (3) They may rejoice in 'receiving of the truth, as he that received the seed into stony places.' [*Matt* 13:20.] (4) They may be in some peace and quiet, in expectation of salvation by Christ, as the foolish virgins were. [*Matt* 25.] (5) All this may be backed and followed with some good measure of reformation, as the Pharisee – 'The Pharisee stood and prayed thus with himself, God, I thank thee that I am not as other men are, extortioners, unjust, adulterers, or even as this publican. I fast twice in the week, I give tithes of all that I possess.' 'The unclean spirit may go out of them.' [*Matt* 12:43; *Luke* 18:11, 12.] (6) This work may seem to be confirmed by some special experiences and 'tastings of the good word of God.' [*Heb* 6:4.]

Fourthly, Hypocrites may have some things very like the saving graces of the Spirit; as (1) They may have a sort of faith, like Simon Magus – 'Then Simon himself believed also: and when he was baptized, he continued with Philip, and wondered, beholding the miracles and signs which were done.' [*Acts* 8:13.] (2) They may have a sort of repentance, and may walk mournfully – 'What profit is it that we have walked mournfully before the Lord of hosts?' [*Mal* 3:14.] (3) They may have a great fear of God, such as Balaam had, who, for a house full of gold, would not go with the messengers of Balak, without leave asked of God and given. [*Num* 22:18.] (4) They have a sort of hope – 'The hypocrite's hope shall perish.' [*Job* 8:13.] (5) They may have some love, as had Herod to John – 'And the king was exceeding sorry; yet for his oath's sake, and for their sakes which sat with him, he would not reject her.' [*Mark* 6:26.] I need not insist, as it is out of all question, they have counterfeits of all saving graces.

Fifthly, They have somewhat like the special communications of God, and the witnessing of His Spirit, and somewhat like 'the powers of the world to come, working powerfully on them, with some flashes of joy arising thence,' as *Heb* 6:4, 5 – 'For it is impossible for those who were once enlightened, and have tasted of the heavenly gift, and were made partakers of the Holy Ghost, and have tasted the good word of God, and the powers of the world to come; if they shall fall away, to renew them again unto repentance.' Notwithstanding of all which, they are but 'almost persuaded,' with Agrippa, to 'become Christians.' [*Acts* 26:28.] It were tedious to speak particularly to each of these things, and to clear it up, that they are all unsound; I shall point out some few things, wherein a truly renewed man, who is in Christ, doth differ from hypocrites and reprobates.

1. Whatever changes be in hypocrites, yet their heart is not changed, and made new. The new heart is only given to the elect, when they are converted and brought under the bond of the covenant – 'I will give them one heart, and one way, that they may fear me for ever.' 'A new heart will I give you, and a new spirit will I put within you; and I will take away the stony heart out of your flesh, and I will give you an heart of flesh.' [*Jer* 32:39; *Ezek* 36:26.] Hypocrites never apprehended Christ as the only satisfying good in all the world, for which with joy they would quit all; for then the kingdom of God were entered into them. 'The kingdom of heaven is

like unto a treasure hid in a field; the which when a man hath found, he hideth, and for joy thereof goeth and selleth all that he hath, and buyeth that field.' [*Matt* 13:44.] The truly renewed man dare, and can upon good ground say, and hath a testimony of it from on high, that his heart hath been changed in taking up with Christ, and hath been led out after Him, as the only enriching treasure, in whom 'to be found he accounteth all things else loss and dung.' [*Phil* 3:8, 9.]

2. Whatever reformation or profession hypocrites attain unto, as it cometh not from a new heart, and pure principle of zeal for God, so it is always for some wicked or base end; as, 'to be seen of men' [*Matt* 6:5], or to evade and shun some outward strait, to be freed from God's wrath, and the trouble of their own conscience – 'Wherefore have we fasted, say they, and Thou seest not? wherefore have we afflicted our soul, and Thou takest no knowledge?' [*Is* 58:3.] 'What profit is it that we have kept His ordinances, and that we have walked mournfully before the Lord of Hosts?' [*Mal* 3:14.] In testimony of this, they never have respect to all known commands, else they should 'never be ashamed' [*Ps* 119:6]; nor do they, without guile in their own heart, resolve against every known iniquity, else they were free of heart-condemnings, and so might justly 'have confidence before God.' [1 *John* 3:21.] If from a principle of love unto, and of zeal for Christ, and for a right end, they did, in ever so small a degree, confess and profess Him, Christ were obliged by His own word to confess them before His Father. [*Matt* 10:32.]

3. Whatever length hypocrites advance in that work, by which people are led on unto Christ, yet they never 'seek first the kingdom of God and His righteousness.'

[*Matt* 6:33.] 'The one thing that is necessary,' namely, Christ's friendship and fellowship, is never their *one thing* and heart-satisfying choice, else that 'better part would never be taken from them.' [*Luke* 10:42.]

4. Whatever counterfeits of grace are in hypocrites, yet they are all produced without any saving work of the Spirit of Christ; and it is enough to exclude them from the benefit of this mark, that they are never denied to these things, nor emptied of them, but still do rest on them as their Saviour, so that they 'submit not unto the righteousness of God' [*Rom* 10:3]; and that is enough to keep them at a distance from Christ, who will never mend that old garment of hypocrites with His fine new linen, nor 'put His new wine in these old bottles.' [*Matt* 9:16, 17.]

5. We may say, Let hypocrites, reprobates, or atheists have what they can, they want the three great essentials of religion and true Christianity – (1) They are not broken in heart, and emptied of their own righteousness, so as to loathe themselves. Such 'lost ones Christ came to seek and save.' [*Luke* 19:10.] (2) They never took up Christ Jesus as the only treasure and jewel that can enrich and satisfy; and therefore, have never cordially agreed unto God's device in the covenant, and so are not worthy of Him; neither hath the kingdom of God savingly entered into their heart – 'The kingdom of heaven is like unto a treasure hid in a field; the which when a man hath found, he hideth, and for joy thereof selleth all that he hath, and buyeth that field.' [*Matt* 13:44.] (3) They never in earnest close with Christ's whole yoke without exception, judging all His 'will just and good, holy and spiritual' [*Rom* 7:12]; and therefore no rest is given to them by Christ – 'Take my yoke upon you, and ye shall find rest unto your souls.' [*Matt* 11:29.] Therefore, whosoever

thou art, who can lay clear and just claim to these three aforesaid things, Thou art beyond the reach of all atheists, hypocrites, and reprobates in the world, as having answered the great ends and intents of the law and gospel.

CHAPTER VI

Reasons why some believers doubt their interest in Christ

I DOUBTS BECAUSE OF PREVAILING SIN ANSWERED

Objection: I am clear sometimes, I think, to lay claim to that mark of the new creature; yet at other times sin doth so prevail over me, that I am made to question all the work within me.

Answer: It is much to be lamented, that people professing the name of Christ should be so abused and enslaved by transgression, as many are. Yet, in answer to the objection, if it be seriously proposed, we say, The saints are found in Scripture justly laying claim to God and His covenant, when iniquity did prevail over them, as we find – 'Iniquities prevail against me; as for our transgressions, Thou shalt purge them away.' [*Ps* 65:3.] Thus Paul thanks God through Christ, even while lamenting that a law in his members leads him captive unto sin. [*Rom* 7:25.] But for the right understanding, and safe application of such truths, we must make a difference betwixt gross out-breakings and ordinary infirmities or heart-evils, or sins that come unawares upon a man, without forethought or any deliberation. As for the former sort, it is hard for a man, whilst he is under the power of them, to see his gracious change, although it be in him: and very hard to draw any comfort from it, until the man be in some measure recovered, and begin seriously to resent such sins, and to resolve against them. We find David calling himself God's servant, quickly after his numbering of God's people; but he was then under the serious resentment of his sin – 'And David's heart smote him after he had numbered the people. David said unto the Lord, I have sinned greatly in that I have done: and now I beseech Thee, O Lord, take away the iniquity of Thy servant, for I have done foolishly.' [2 *Sam* 24:10.] Jonah layeth claim to God as his Master under his rebellion; but he is then repenting it, and in a spirit of revenge against himself for his sin.' [*Jonah* 1:9–12.]

Next, as for those sins of infirmity, and daily incursions of heart-evils, such as those whereof (it is like) Paul doth complain, we shall draw out some things from the seventh chapter to the Romans, upon which Paul maintains his interest in Christ, and if you can apply them it is well. (1) When Paul finds that he doth much fail, and cannot reach conformity to God's law, he doth not blame the law, as being too strict, so that men cannot keep it, as hypocrites use to speak; but he blames himself as being carnal; and he saith of the law, 'that it is good, holy, and spiritual.' [*Rom* 7:12, 14.] (2) He can say, he failed of a good which he intended, and did outshoot himself, and he had often honestly resolved against the sin into which he fell –'For that which I do I allow not; for what I would, that do I not; but what I hate, that do I. For I know that in me (that is, in my flesh) dwelleth no good thing: for to will is present with me; but how to perform that which is good I find not. For the good that I would I do not; but the evil which I would not, that I do.' [*Rom* 7:15, 18, 19.] (3) He saith that the prevailing of sin over him is his burden, so that he judgeth himself wretched because of such a body of death, from which he longeth to be delivered. [*Rom* 7:24.] (4) He saith, that whilst he is under the power and law of sin, there is somewhat in the bottom of his heart opposing it, although overcome by it, which would be another way, and when that gets the upper hand it is a delightsome thing. [*Rom* 7:22–25.] Upon these things he 'thanks God in Christ that there is no condemnation to them who are in Christ Jesus, who walk not after the flesh, but after the Spirit.' [*Rom* 8:1.] Now, then, see if you can lay claim to these things. (1) If you blame yourself, and approve the law, whilst you fail. (2) If you can say that you often resolve against sin honestly, and without known guile; and do so resolve the contrary good before the evil break in upon you. (3) If you can say, that you are so far exercised with your failings, as to judge yourself wretched because of such things, and a body of death, which is the root and fountain of such things. (4) If you can say, that there is a party within you opposing these evils, which would be at the right way, and, as it were, is in its element when it is in God's way, it is well: only be advised not to take rest, until, in some good measure, you be rid of the ground of this objection, or, at least, until you can very clearly say, you are waging war with these things. Now, a good help against the prevailing power of sin is to cleave close to Christ Jesus by faith, which, as it is a desirable part of sanctification, and a high degree of conformity to God's will, and most subservient unto His design in the gospel, should be much endeavoured by people, as a work pleasing unto God – 'The life which I now live in the flesh, I live by the faith of the Son of God, who loved me, and gave Himself for me. I do not frustrate the grace of God.' [*Gal* 2:21.] 'This is the work of God, that ye believe on Him whom He hath sent.' [*John* 6:29.] This is the ready way to draw life and sap from Christ, the blessed root, for fruitfulness in all cases, as in *John* 15:4, 5 – 'Abide in Me, and I in you; as the branch cannot bear fruit of itself, except it abide in the vine; no more can ye, except ye abide in Me. I am the vine, ye are the branches: he that abideth in Me, and I in him, the same bringeth forth much fruit: for without Me ye can do nothing.'

2 DOUBTS ARISING FROM A WANT OF CHRISTIAN EXPERIENCE ANSWERED

Objection: I do not partake of those special communications of God mentioned in the Scripture, and of those actings and outgoings of His Spirit, of which gracious people are often speaking, and whereunto they attain. The want of these things maketh me much suspect my state.

Answer: I shall shortly point out some of these excellent communications, and I hope, upon a right discovery of them, there will be but small ground left for the jealous complaints of many gracious people.

1. Besides those convictions of the Spirit of God, which usually usher Christ's way into the souls of men, and those also which afterwards do ordinarily attend them, there is a seal of the Spirit of God spoken of in Scripture, the principal thing whereof is the sanctifying work of the Holy Ghost, imprinting the drafts and lineaments of God's image and revealed will upon a man, as a seal or signet doth leave the impression and stamp of its likeness upon the thing sealed. So it is – 'The foundation of God standeth sure, having this seal, The Lord knoweth them that are His; and, Let every one that nameth the name of Christ depart from iniquity.' [2 *Tim* 2:19.] And thus I conceive the seal to be called a witness – 'He that believeth

hath the witness in himself' [1 *John* 5:10]; that is, the grounds upon which an interest in Christ is to be made out and proved, are in every believer; for he hath somewhat of the sanctifying work of God's Spirit in him, which is a sure, although not always a clear and manifest witness.

3. There is *communion* with God much talked of among Christians, whereby they understand the sensible presence of God refreshing the soul exceedingly. But if we speak properly, communion with God is a mutual interest between God and a man, who hath closed with him in Christ. It is a commonness, or a common interest between God and a man: not only as a man interested in God Himself, but in all that is the Lord's; so the Lord hath a special interest in the man, and also all that belongs to him. There is a communion between husband and wife, whereby they have a special interest in each other's persons, goods, and concerns: so it is here. There is such a communion with God; He is our God, and all things are ours, because He is ours. This communion with God all true believers have at all times, as we shall show afterwards. I grant there is an actual improvement of that communion, whereby men do boldly approach unto God and converse with Him as their God with holy familiarity; especially in worship, when the soul doth converse with a living God, partaking of the divine nature, growing like unto Him, and sweetly travelling through His attributes, and, with some confidence of interest, viewing these things as the man's own goods and property: this we call communion with God in ordinances. This indeed is not so ordinarily nor frequently made out to men, and all His people do not equally partake of it: and it is true that what is in God, goeth not out for the benefit of the man to his apprehension equally at all times: yet certainly communion with God,

properly so called, namely, that commonness of interest between God and a man who is savingly in covenant with Him, doth always stand firm and sure; and so much of communion with God in ordinances have all believers, as that their heart converseth with a living God there, now and then, and is, in some measure, changed into that same image; and there needeth not be any further doubt about it.

3. There is also *fellowship* with God, which is often mistaken amongst believers. If by fellowship be meant the walking in our duty, as in the sight of a living God, who seeth and heareth us, and is witness to all our carriage, it is a thing common unto all gracious men; they all have it habitually, and in design – 'I have set the Lord always before me.' [*Ps* 16:8.] Yea, and often they have it actually in exercise, when their spirit is in any good frame: they walk as if they saw God standing by them, and have some thought of His favour through Christ – 'Truly our fellowship is with the Father, and with His Son Jesus Christ.' [1 *John* 1:3.] If by *fellowship* we mean a sweet, refreshing, familiar, sensible, conversing with God, which doth delight and refresh the soul (besides what the conscience of duty doth); it is then a walking in the light of His countenance, and a good part of sensible presence: and although it seemeth Enoch had much of it, whilst it is said, 'He walked with God' [*Gen* 5:24]; yet it is not so ordinary as the former, nor so common to all Christians; for here the soul is filled as with marrow and fatness, following hard after its Guide, and singularly upheld by His right hand – 'My soul shall be satisfied as with marrow and fatness: and my mouth shall praise Thee with joyful lips. My soul followeth hard after Thee, Thy right hand upholdeth me.' [*Ps* 63:5, 8.]

4. There is also *access* unto God; and this I take to be

the removing of obstructions out of the way between a man and God, so that the man is admitted to come near. We are said to have access to a great person when the doors are cast open, the guards removed from about him, and we are admitted to come close to him: so it is here. Now this access, in Scripture, is sometimes taken for Christ's preparing of the way, the removing of enmity between God and sinners, so as men now have an open way to come unto God through Christ – 'For through Him we both have an access by one Spirit unto the Father.' [*Eph* 2:18.] Sometimes it is taken for the actual improvement of that access purchased by Christ, when a man finds all obstructions and differences which do ordinarily fall in between him and God removed: God does not act towards him as a stranger, keeping up Himself from him, or frowning on him, but the man is admitted to 'come even to His seat.' [*Job* 23:3.] Of the want of which he complains, whilst he saith, 'Behold, I go forward, but He is not there; and backward, but I cannot perceive Him; on the left hand, where He doth work, but I cannot behold Him; He hideth Himself on the right hand, that I cannot see Him.' [*Job* 23:8, 9.] The first sort of access is common to all believers: they are brought near by the blood of the covenant; and are no more afar off, as the deadly enmity between God and them is removed; but access in the other sense is dispensed more according to the Lord's absolute sovereignty and pleasure, and it is left in the power of believers to obstruct it to themselves, until it please the Lord mercifully and freely to grant it unto them again; so it is up and down; and there needs be no question as to a man's state about it.

5. There is also *liberty* before God; and this properly is freedom, or free speaking unto God. Many do much

question their state, because of the want of this now and then, since the Scripture hath said, 'Where the Spirit of the Lord is, there is liberty' [2 *Cor* 3:17]; but they do unjustly confine that liberty spoken of there unto this free speaking before God. I grant, where the Spirit of the Lord savingly discovers God's will in the Scriptures to a man, there is liberty from any obligation to the ceremonial law, and from the condemning power of the moral law, and from much of that gross darkness and ignorance which is naturally on men's hearts as a veil hiding Christ in the gospels from them. I grant also, that sometimes even this liberty, which is a free communing with God, and 'ordering of our cause before Him, and filling of our mouths with arguments' [*Job* 23:4], is granted to the godly, but not as liberty taken in the former senses. Although the Lord hath obliged Himself to 'pour out the spirit of prayer upon all the house of David' [*Zech* 12:10], in some measure, yet this communication of the Spirit, which we call *liberty* or *free speaking* unto God, dependeth much on the Lord's absolute pleasure, when, and in what measure to allow it. This liberty, which we call *freedom* or *free speaking* with God in prayer, is sometimes much withdrawn as to any great confidence in the time of prayer, at least until it draw towards the close of it. It standeth much in a vivacity of the understanding to take up the case which a man is to speak before God, so that he can order his cause; and next there be words, or verbal expressions, elegant, suitable, and very emphatical, or powerful and pithy. There is also joined a fervency of spirit in prayer, of which the Scripture speaks; the soul is warm and bended, and very intent. There is also ordinarily in this liberty a special melting of the heart often joined with a great measure of the 'spirit of grace and supplication.' [*Zech* 12:10.] So the soul is poured out before God as for a first-born. Such is the liberty which many saints get before God, whilst, in much brokenness of heart and fervency of spirit, they are admitted to speak their mind fully to God, as a living God, noticing (at least) their prayer. Sometimes this liberty is joined with confidence: and then it is not only a free, but also a bold speaking before God. It is that 'boldness with confidence' [*Eph* 3:12] – 'In whom we have boldness and access with confidence, by the faith of Him.' This is more rarely imparted unto men than the former, yet it is ordinary: it hath in it, besides what we mentioned before, some influence of the Spirit upon faith, making it put forth some vigorous acting in prayer. There is a sweet mournful frame of spirit, by which a man poureth out his heart in God's bosom, and with some confidence of His favour and good-will, pleadeth his cause before Him as a living God; and this is all the sensible presence that many saints do attain unto. There is no ground of doubt concerning a man's state in the point of liberty before God, in this last sense, because there is nothing essential to the making up of a gracious state here: some have it, some want it; some have it at some times, and not at others; so that it is much up and down; yet I may say gracious men may do much, by a very ordinary influence, in contributing towards the attaining and retaining, or keeping of such a frame of spirit.

6. There is also an *influence*, or breathing of the Spirit. This gracious influence (for of such only do I now speak) is either ordinary: and this is the operation of the Holy Spirit on the soul, and the habits of grace there, whereby they are still kept alive, and in some exercise and acting, although not very discernible. This influence, I conceive,

doth always attend believers, and is that 'keeping and watering night and day, and every moment,' promised in *Is* 27:3. Or, this influence is more singular and special, and is the same to a gracious, although a withered soul, as the 'wind and breath to the dry bones' [*Ezek* 37:9, 10]; putting them in good case, and 'as the dew or rain to the grass,' or newly-mown field and parched ground. [*Ps* 72:6.] Such influence is meant by the 'blowing of the south-wind, making the spices to flow out.' [*Cant* 4:16.] When the Spirit moveth thus, there is an edge put upon the graces of God in the soul, and they are made to act more vigorously. This is the 'enlarging of the heart,' by which 'a man doth run in the ways of God.' [*Ps* 119:32.] This influence is more discernible than the former, and not so ordinarily communicated. Also here sometimes the wind bloweth more upon one grace, and sometimes more discernibly upon another, and often upon many of the graces together; and, according to the lesser or greater measure of this influence, the soul acteth more or less vigorously towards God; and since faith is a created grace in the soul, this influence of the Spirit is upon it, sometimes less, sometimes more, and accordingly is the assurance of faith small or great.

7. There is the *hearing of prayer*, often spoken of in Scripture; and many vex themselves about it, alleging that they know nothing of it experimentally. I grant there is a favourable hearing of prayer; but we must remember it is twofold. Either (1) It is such as a man is simply to believe by way of argument on scriptural grounds; as if I had fled unto Christ, and approached unto God in Him, praying according to His will, not regarding iniquity in my heart, exercising faith about the thing I pray for absolutely or conditionally, according to the nature of the

thing and promises concerning it; I am obliged to believe that God heareth my prayer, and will give what is good, according to these scriptures – 'Whatsoever ye shall ask in my name, I will do it.' [*John* 14:13.] 'This is our confidence, that whatsoever we ask according to His will He heareth us.' [1 *John* 5:14.] 'Believe that ye receive them, and ye shall have them.' [*Mark* 11:24.] 'If I regard iniquity in my heart, the Lord will not hear me.' [*Ps* 66:18.] Then, if I regard not iniquity, I may believe that He doth hear me.' Or, (2) A man doth sensibly perceive that God heareth his prayer; it is made out to his heart, without any syllogistical deduction. Such a hearing of prayer Hannah obtained – 'Her countenance was no more sad.' [1 *Sam* 1:18.] Surely the Lord did breathe upon her faith, and made her believe she was heard: she could not make it out by any argument; for she had not grounds whereupon to build the premises of the argument, according to Scripture, in that particular: God did stamp it some way upon her heart sensibly, and so made her believe it. This is but rarely granted, especially in cases clearly deducible in Scripture; therefore people ought to be much occupied in exercising their faith about the other, and ought to leave it to God to give of this latter what He pleaseth. A man's gracious state should not be brought into debate upon the account of such hearing of prayer.

8. There is *assurance* of God's favour by the witnessing of our own spirits; which assurance is adduced by way of argument syllogistically, thus – Whosoever believeth on Christ shall never perish: but I do believe on Christ, therefore I shall never perish. Whoso hath respect unto all God's commandments shall never be ashamed; but I have respect unto all His commandments; therefore I shall never be ashamed. I say, by reasoning thus, and com-

paring spiritual things with spiritual things, a man may attain unto a good certainty of his gracious state. It is supposed [1 *John* 3:18, 19] that by loving the brethren in deed and in truth, we may 'assure our hearts before God'; and that a man may rejoice upon the testimony of a good conscience. [2 *Cor* 1:12.] A man may have 'confidence towards God, if his heart do not condemn him.' [1 *John* 3:21.] We may then attain unto some assurance, although not full assurance, by the witness of our own spirits. I do not deny, that in this witnessing of our spirits concerning assurance, there is some concurrence of the Spirit of God: but, I conceive, there needeth but a very ordinary influence, without which we can do nothing. Now this assurance, such as it is, may be reached by intelligent believers, who keep a good conscience in their walk. So, I hope, there needs be no debate about it, as to a man's gracious state; for if a man will clear himself of heart-condemnings, he will speedily reach this assurance.

9. There is a *witnessing of God's Spirit*, mentioned as 'bearing witness with our spirit that we are the children of God.' [*Rom* 8:16.] This operation of the Spirit is best understood, if we produce any syllogism by which our spirit doth witness our sonship; as for example, Whosoever loveth the brethren is passed from death to life, and consequently is in Christ: but I love the brethren; therefore I am passed from death to life. Here there is a threefold operation of the Spirit, or three operations rather. The first is a beam of divine light upon the first proposition, evincing the divine authority of it, as the word of God. The Spirit of the Lord must witness the divinity of the Scriptures, and that it is the infallible word of God, far beyond all other arguments that can be used for it. The second operation is a glorious beam of light from the

Spirit, shining upon the second proposition, and so upon His own graces in the soul, discovering them to be true graces, and such as the Scripture calleth so. Thus we are said to 'know by His Spirit the things that are freely given unto us of God.' [1 *Cor* 2:13.] The third operation is connected with the third proposition of the argument, or the conclusion, and this I conceive to be nothing else but an influence upon faith, strengthening it to draw a conclusion of full assurance upon the aforesaid premises.

Now, with submission to others, who have greater light in the Scripture, and more experience of these precious communications, I do conceive the witness of the Spirit, or witnessing of it, which is mentioned, 'The Spirit itself beareth witness with our spirit that we are the children of God' [*Rom* 8:16], is not that first operation upon the first proposition; for that operation is that testimony of the Spirit by which He beareth witness to the divinity of the whole Scripture, and asserts the divine authority of it unto the souls of gracious men; and such an operation may be upon a truth of Scripture, which does not relate to a man's sonship or interest in Christ at all. The Spirit may so shine upon any truth, relating to duty, or any other fundamental truth, impressing the divinity of it upon and unto the soul, and speak nothing relating to a man's interest in Christ. Neither is the third operation of the Spirit, by which He makes faith boldly draw the conclusion, this witnessing of the Spirit; for that operation is nothing else but an influence upon faith, bringing it out to full assurance; but that upon which this full assurance is drawn or put out, is somewhat confirmed and witnessed already. Therefore I conceive the second operation of the Spirit, upon the second proposition, and so upon the graces in the man, is that witness of God's Spirit, that beam of divine light shining upon those graces, whereby they are made very conspicuous to the understanding. That is the witness, the shining so on them is His witnessing: for, only here, in this proposition, and in this operation, doth the Spirit of God prove a co-witness with our spirit: for the main thing wherein lies the witness of our spirit is in the second proposition, and so the Spirit of God witnessing with our spirits is also in that same proposition. So these two witnesses having confirmed and witnessed one and the same thing, namely, the truth and reality of such and such graces in the man, which our own spirit or conscience doth depone according to its knowledge, and the Spirit of the Lord doth certainly affirm and witness to be so, there is a sentence drawn forth, and a conclusion of the man's sonship by the man's faith, breathed upon by the Spirit for that purpose; and this conclusion beareth the full assurance of a man's sonship. It may be presumed that some true saints do not partake of this all their days – 'And deliver them, who through fear of death were all their lifetime subject to bondage.' [*Heb* 2:15.]

10. I speak with the experience of many saints, and, I hope, according to Scripture, if I say there is a communication of the Spirit of God which is sometimes vouchsafed to some of His people that is somewhat besides, if not beyond, that witnessing of a sonship spoken of before. It is a glorious divine manifestation of God unto the soul, shedding abroad God's love in the heart; it is a thing better felt than spoke of: it is no audible voice, but it is a ray of glory filling the soul with God, as He is life, light, love, and liberty, corresponding to that audible voice, 'O man, greatly beloved' [*Dan* 9:23]; putting a man in a transport with this on his heart, 'It is good to be

here.' [*Matt* 17:4.] It is that which went out from Christ to Mary, when He but mentioned her name – 'Jesus saith unto her, Mary. She turned herself, and saith unto Him, Rabboni, which is to say, Master.' [*John* 20:16.] He had spoken some words to her before, and she understood not that it was He: but when He uttereth this one word MARY, there was some admirable divine conveyance and manifestation made out unto her heart, by which she was so satisfyingly filled, that there was no place for arguing and disputing whether or no that was Christ, and if she had any interest in Him. That manifestation wrought faith to itself, and did purchase credit and trust to itself, and was equivalent with, 'Thus saith the Lord.' This is such a glance of glory, that it may in the highest sense be called 'the earnest,' or first-fruits 'of the inheritance' [*Eph* 1:14]; for it is a present, and, as it were, sensible discovery of the holy God, almost wholly conforming the man unto His likeness; so swallowing him up, that he forgetteth all things except the present manifestation. O how glorious is this manifestation of the Spirit! Faith here riseth to so full an assurance, that it resolveth wholly into the sensible presence of God. This is the thing which doth best deserve the title of *sensible presence*; and is not given unto all believers, some whereof, 'are all their days under bondage, and in fear' [*Heb* 2:15]; but here 'love, almost perfect, casteth out fear.' [1 *John* 4:18.] This is so absolutely let out upon the Master's pleasure, and so transient or passing, or quickly gone when it is, that no man may bring his gracious state into debate for want of it.

11. There is what we call *peace*, about which many do vex themselves. This peace is either concerning a man's state, that he is reconciled unto God by Jesus Christ; or it is relating to his present case and condition, that he is

walking so as approved of God, at least so far as there is no quarrel or controversy between God and him threatening a stroke. Both of these are either such in the court of Scripture, and consequently in God's account, or in the court of a man's own conscience. *Peace* with respect to a man's state, as being in Christ, is sure in the court of Scripture and of heaven, when a man doth by faith close with Christ and the new covenant. 'Being justified by faith, we have peace with God.' [*Rom* 5:1.] It being sure and solid in the court of Scripture, it should hold sure in the court of a man's conscience, if it be rightly informed; for, in that case, it still speaks according to Scripture. But because often the conscience is misinformed and in the dark, therefore there is often peace as to a man's state according to Scripture, whilst his conscience threatens the contrary, and doth still condemn, and refuseth to acquit the man, as being reconciled unto God through Christ. In this case, the conscience must be informed, and the man's gracious state made out by the marks of grace, as we showed before; and here the witness of my own spirit will do much to allay the cry of the conscience; and if the Spirit of the Lord join His witness and testimony, the conscience is perfectly satisfied, and proclaimeth peace to the man.

The other *peace*, as to a man's present case or condition, namely, that it is approved of God in a gospel sense, may be awanting, and justly wanting, although the peace concerning a man's state be sure. This peace as to a man's case and condition, is either such in the court of Scripture, and this is when a man is not regarding iniquity, and respecting the commands of God without exception: then the Scripture saith, he stands in an even place, and he need fear no stated quarrel between God and him in order to a temporary stroke: and when it is thus, his conscience should also acquit him that same way, and would do so if it were rightly informed. But because the conscience is often in the dark, therefore a man may be alarmed with evil in the court of conscience, as if he were justly to expect a stroke from God because of his sin, and some quarrel God hath at him, although He intend salvation for him. This is enough to keep a man in disquiet, and to prohibit him from the rejoicing allowed him whilst he is walking in his integrity; therefore a man must here also inform his conscience, and receive no accusations or condemnings from it, unless it make them clear by Scripture. At that bar let every man stand, both as to his state, and his condition or case; let him appeal from all other courts to that, and not receive any indictment, unless conformed to the truth of God, by which the conscience is to be regulated in all things. And if this were well looked unto, there would not be so many groundless suspicions amongst the Lord's people, either as to their state or their condition, upon every thought which entereth their mind.

12. There is the *joy* of the Holy Ghost; and this is when the Spirit breathes upon our rejoicing in God, which is a grace very little in exercise with many, and maketh it set out sensibly and vigorously; and when He excites and stirs the passion of joy and of delight in the soul, so that there is an unspeakable and glorious joy in the soul, in the apprehension of God's friendship and nearness unto him – 'In whom though now ye see Him not, yet believing, ye rejoice with joy unspeakable and full of glory.' [1 *Peter* 1:8.] This joy followeth upon peace, and peace followeth upon righteousness – 'The kingdom of God is righteousness and peace, and joy in the Holy Ghost.' [*Rom* 14:17.] This joy will in general not fail to be according

to the measure of the assurance of faith, as 1 *Peter* 1:8 – 'In whom believing ye rejoice.' So that the removal of mistakes about other things will allay doubts as to this.

Now, because some of these excellent communications of the Spirit, after they are gone, are brought into question as delusions of Satan: for vindication of them, we say that the special operations of God's Spirit in any high degree, usually are communicated to people after much brokenness of spirit – 'Make me to hear joy and gladness, that the bones which Thou hast broken may rejoice' [*Ps* 51:8]; after singular pains in religious duty – 'And I set my face unto the Lord God to seek by prayer and supplication, with fasting, and sackcloth, and ashes: and whiles I was speaking and praying, and confessing my sin, the man Gabriel whom I had seen in the vision at the beginning, being caused to fly swiftly, touched me' [*Dan* 9:3, 21]; or in time of great suffering for righteousness – 'Rejoice, inasmuch as ye are partakers of Christ's sufferings, that when His glory shall be revealed, ye may be glad also with exceeding joy. If ye be reproached for the name of Christ, happy are ye, for the Spirit of glory and of God resteth upon you' [1 *Peter* 4:14]; or if they break in as the rain that waiteth not for man, then they do so humble and abase the person – 'Woe is me, for I am undone, because I am a man of unclean lips; for mine eyes have seen the King, the Lord of hosts' [*Is* 6:5]; and there are found so many evidences of grace in the man – 'The Spirit itself beareth witness with our spirit, that we are the children of God' [*Rom* 8:16]; or these things do so provoke unto holiness, and to have every thing answerable and conformable to these manifestations of God – 'Let every one that nameth the name of Christ, depart from iniquity.' [2 *Tim* 2:19.] The person under them loathes all things besides God's friendship and fellowship – 'Peter said unto Jesus, Lord, it is good for us to be here.' [*Matt* 17:4.] And these things carry on them and with them so much authority and divine superscription, whilst they are in the soul, that afterwards they do appear sufficiently to be special communications of God, and singular gracious operations of His Spirit, and no delusion of 'Satan transforming himself into an angel of light' [2 *Cor* 11:14]; nor such common flashes of the Spirit as may afterwards admit of irrecoverable apostasy from God – 'For it is impossible for those who were once enlightened, and have tasted of the heavenly gift, and were made partakers of the Holy Ghost, and have tasted the good word of God, and the powers of the world to come, if they shall fall away, to renew them again unto repentance.' [*Heb* 6:4, 5, 6.]

3 CONCLUSION

Now, then, to conclude this part of the work that relates to the trial: I say to all those who complain of the want of the precious outpourings of the Spirit, (1) Bless God if you want nothing essential for the making out of a saving interest in Christ. God hath given unto you Christ Jesus, the greatest gift He had; and since your heart is laid out for Him, He will, with Him, give you all things that are good for you in their season. (2) I do believe, upon a strict search and trial, after you have understood the communications of the Spirit, you are not so great a stranger to many things as you suspected yourselves to be. But (3) Remember, the promises of life and of peace with God, are nowhere in Scripture made unto those special things whereof you allege the want: the promises are made unto faith, followed with holiness; and it may be presumed, that many heirs of glory do not in this life partake of some of these things, but 'are in bondage all their days through fear of death' [*Heb* 2:15]; so that there shall be no mistake about these things; we may seek after them, but God is free to give or withhold them. (4) Many do seek after such manifestations before they give credit by faith unto God's word. He hath borne record that there is life enough for men in Christ Jesus; and if men would by believing, set to their seal that God is true, they should partake of more of these excellent things. (5) I may say many have not honourable apprehensions and thoughts of the Spirit of God, whose proper work it is to put forth the aforesaid noble operations. They do not adore Him as God, but vex, grieve, quench, and resist Him: and many people, complaining of the want of these things, are not at the pains to seek the Spirit in His outgoings, and few do set themselves apart for such precious receptions: therefore be at more pains in religion, given more credit to His word, and esteem more highly the grace of the Spirit of God, and so you may find more of these excellent things.

PART II

How to attain a saving interest in Christ

Introduction

Having, in the former part of this Treatise, put every man's state to the trial, it now remains that, in this following part, we give advice to those who neither can nor dare lay claim to the marks formerly mentioned.

QUESTION TWO

What shall they do who want[1] the marks of a true and saving interest in Christ, already spoken of, and neither can nor dare pretend unto them?

Answer: If men do not discover in themselves the marks of a saving interest in Christ, spoken of before, then it is their duty, and the duty of all that hear the gospel, personally and heartily to close with God's device of saving sinners by Christ Jesus, and thus to secure their state.

[1] want = lack.

CHAPTER I

Some things premised for the information of the ignorant

For the better understanding of this, we shall premise some things for the information of those who are more ignorant, and then speak more directly to the thing. As for the things to be premised:

1. The Lord did, at the beginning, out of His bounty, make a covenant with man in Adam – 'And the Lord God commanded the man, saying, Of every tree in the garden thou mayest freely eat; but of the tree of the knowledge of good and evil, thou shalt not eat of it; for in the day that thou eatest thereof thou shalt surely die.' [*Gen* 2:16, 17.] And He gave the man ability to abide in that covenant – 'God hath made man upright' [*Eccles* 7:29]; but man, by eating of that forbidden fruit, did break that covenant – 'They, like Adam, have transgressed the covenant' [*Hos* 6:7]; and made it void for ever, and involved himself in misery thereby – 'By the deeds of the law, there shall no flesh be justified in His sight' [*Rom* 3:20]; 'As by one man sin entered into the world, and death by sin; and so death passed upon all men, for that all have sinned.' [*Rom* 5:12.]

2. The Lord did most freely, from everlasting, purpose and intend to save men another way, namely, by Christ Jesus, and the covenant of grace, in which He intended reconciliation with the elect through Christ Jesus, God and Man, born of a woman, in due time to make this agreement effectual. And this device of satisfying His own

justice, and saving of the elect by Christ, He did at first intimate to our parents in paradise, saying, 'That the seed of the woman shall bruise the serpent's head.' [*Gen* 3:15.] And the Lord hath in all generations made this known to His church.

3. The Lord hath in all ages covenanted to be the reconciled God of all those who, by their subjection to His ordinances, did profess their satisfaction with this device, and oblige themselves to acquiesce in the same, and to seek salvation by Christ Jesus, as God doth offer Him in the gospel; so all the people of Israel are called the Lord's people, and are said to avouch Him to be their God, and He doth avouch them to be His people – 'Thou hast avouched the Lord this day to be thy God, and to walk in His ways, and to keep His statutes, and His commandments, and His judgments, and to hearken unto His voice; and the Lord hath avouched thee this day to be His peculiar people, as He hath promised thee, and that thou shouldest keep all His commandments.' [*Deut* 26:17, 18.] Yea, the Lord doth also engage Himself to be the God of the seed and children of those who do so subject themselves to His ordinances. The *covenant* is said to be made between God and all the people, young and old, present and not present that day [*Deut* 29:10–15.]; and all are appointed to come under some seal of that covenant, as was enjoined to Abraham. [*Gen* 17:10.] Not only was it so in the Old Testament, but it is so in the New Testament also. The Lord makes offer of Himself to be our God in Christ Jesus; and the people professing their satisfaction in that offer, and in testimony thereof subjecting themselves unto the ordinances, they are reckoned a covenanted people, and are joined unto His church in thousands, receiving a seal of the covenant, without any

further particular previous trial – 'Then Peter said unto them, Repent, and be baptized, every one of you, in the name of Jesus Christ, for the remission of sins. Then they that gladly received the word were baptized; and the same day there were added unto them about three thousand souls.' [*Acts* 2:38, 41.]

4. Many deal treacherously with God in this covenant – 'Nevertheless, they did flatter Him with their mouth, and they lied unto Him with their tongues; for their heart was not right with Him, neither were they steadfast in His covenant.' [*Ps* 78:36, 37.] And although they profess their estimation of Christ the Saviour, and their heart-satisfaction with that device of saving sinners by Him, and having the image of God restored by Him in them; yet their heart is not right with God, and they do content themselves with an empty title of being in a sealed covenant with God: 'Abraham is our father,' say they. [*John* 8:39.] For although the Lord obligeth every man, who professeth his satisfaction with Christ Jesus, the devised ransom, to be cordial and sincere herein; and only to those who are so doth He make out the spiritual promises of the covenant, they only being privileged to be the sons of God who do really receive Christ [*John* 1:12]; yet the Lord doth permit many to profess their closing with Him in Christ, both in the Old and New Testament, whilst their heart is not engaged; and He doth admit them to be members of His church, granting unto them the use of ordinances, and many other external mercies and privileges denied unto the heathen, who are not in covenant with Him.

5. Although the greater part of people do foolishly fancy that they have closed with God in Christ Jesus sincerely and heartily; or, at least, they do, without any

ground or warrant, promise a new heart to themselves before they depart this life; yet there be but very few who do really and cordially close with God in Christ Jesus as He is offered in the gospel: and so there be but very few saved, as is clear – 'Strait is the gate and narrow is the way which leadeth unto life, and few there be who find it' [*Matt* 7:14]; 'Many are called, but few are chosen.' [*Matt* 20:16.] If people would believe this, it might help to alarm them.

6. Although none at all do cordially close with God in Christ Jesus, and acquiesce in that ransom found out by God, except only such as are elected – 'But the election hath obtained it, and the rest were blinded' [*Rom* 11:7] – and whose hearts the Lord doth sovereignly determine to that blessed choice – 'No man can come to Me, except the Father, which hath sent Me, draw him' [*John* 6:44]; yet the Lord hath left it as a duty upon people who hear this gospel, to close with His offer of salvation through Christ Jesus, as if it were in their power to do it; and the Lord, through these commands and exhortations, wherein He obliged men to the thing, doth convey life and strength to the elect, and doth therein convey the new heart unto them, which pointeth kindly towards this new device of saving sinners, and towards Christ in His covenant relations; for it is the Lord's mind, in these commands and invitations, to put people on some duty, with which He useth to concur for accomplishing that business between Him and them: so then, it is a *coming* on our part, and yet a *drawing* on His part; 'No man can come to Me, except the Father, which hath sent Me, draw him.' [*John* 6:44.] It is a *drawing* on His part, and a *running* on our part – 'Draw me, we will run after Thee.' [*Cant* 1:4.] It is an *approaching* on our part, and yet a 'choosing and

causing to approach' on His part. [*Ps* 65:4.] It is a *believing* or *receiving* on our part – 'But as many as received Him, to them gave He power to become the sons of God, even to them that believe on His name'; and yet 'it is given us to believe.' [*John* 1:12; *Phil* 1:29.]

CHAPTER II

What it is to close with God's Gospel plan of saving sinners by Christ Jesus, and the duty of so doing

Having premised these things, I say, if men do not find in themselves the marks of a saving interest in Christ, spoken of in the former part of the treatise; then, for securing their state, they ought forthwith, with all diligence, personally and heartily to accept of and close with God's plan of saving sinners by Christ Jesus, held out in the gospel.

In handling of this we shall show –

1. What it is to accept of and close with that noble plan.
2. That it is the necessary duty of those who would be in favour with God and secure their souls.
3. What is previously required of those who perform this duty.
4. What are the qualifications and properties of this duty, if rightly managed.
5. What are the native consequences of it, if it be performed aright.

I WHAT IT IS TO ACCEPT OF, AND CLOSE WITH, THE GOSPEL OFFER

1. As for the *first*, What it is to close with God's plan of saving sinners by Christ Jesus, held out in the gospel. Here we must remember as we showed before, that at first God willed man to abide in His favour, by holding fast his first integrity in which he was created; but man

by his transgression lost God's favour, made void that covenant of works, and put himself into an utter incapacity to regain the Lord's friendship, which he had lost by his sin, and to rescue himself from the curse and wrath now due to him for sin, or any way to procure his own salvation: but the Lord hath freely manifested another way of repairing man's lost estate, namely, by sending His Son Christ Jesus in the flesh, to satisfy His justice for the sins of the elect, and to restore in them His image, now defaced, and to bring them unto glory; and He hath made open proclamation in the church, that whosoever will lay aside all thoughts of saving themselves by the covenant of works, or inherent righteousness, and will agree heartily to be saved by Christ Jesus, they shall be restored to a better condition than formerly man was in, and shall be saved. So then, to close with God's plan of saving sinners by Christ Jesus, is to quit and renounce all thoughts of help or salvation by our own righteousness, and to agree unto this way which God hath found out: it is to value and highly esteem Christ Jesus as the treasure sufficient to enrich poor sinners; and with the heart to believe this record, that there is life enough in Him for men: it is to approve this plan and acquiesce in it, as the only way to true happiness: it is to point towards this Mediator, as God holdeth Him out in the gospel, with a desire to lay the stress of our whole state on Him. This is that which is called *faith* or *believing*, the 'receiving of Christ,' or 'believing on His name.' [*John* 1:12.] This is that 'believing on the Lord Jesus Christ,' commanded to the jailer for his safety. [*Acts* 16:31.] This agreeth to all the descriptions of justifying faith in the Scripture. This answers to the type of looking to the 'brazen serpent lifted up in the wilderness' [*John* 3:14, 15]; and this is supposed in all those ordinary actings of faith to which promises are annexed in the Scripture; and will be found in all who have got the new heart from God, and it will be found in none else.

2 THIS THE DUTY OF THOSE WHO WOULD BE SAVED

As to the *second* thing, namely, That this is the necessary duty of all such as would be in favour with God and secure their souls; it appeareth thus:

1. This closing with God's plan or believing in Christ, is commanded everywhere in Scripture by the Lord as the condition of the new covenant, giving right and title unto all the spiritual blessings of the same; for it is, upon the matter, the receiving of Christ. This is commanded, when God bids 'men come and buy,' that is, appropriate all, by closing with that device. [*Is* 55:1.] 'Come unto me, all ye that labour and are heavy laden, and I will give you rest.' [*Matt* 11:28.] The *weary* are commanded to come unto Him thus, for their rest – 'This is His Commandment, that we should believe on the name of His Son Jesus Christ.' [1 *John* 3:23.] This is enough to prove it a duty incumbent. But further, it is such a duty as only gives right and title to a sonship; for only they who receive Him are privileged to be sons – 'But as many as received Him, to them gave He power to become the sons of God, even to them that believe on His name.' [*John* 1:12.]

2. It appears to be the necessary duty of all, thus: No less than this doth give an opportunity for God, offering Himself to be our God in Christ; and no less than this doth answer our profession, as we are in covenant with

Him, as members of His visible church. The Lord offereth to be our God in Christ; if we do not close with the offer, laying aside all thoughts of other ways by which we may attain to happiness, we give no opportunity to Him. He saith – 'This is my beloved Son, in whom I am well pleased, hear ye Him.' [*Matt* 17:5.] If we close not with the offer, we give no answer unto God. Moreover, we are all 'baptized in the name of the Lord Jesus Christ, for the remission of sins.' [*Acts* 2:38.] Now, unless we close with Christ, as aforesaid, we falsify that profession: therefore, since this is the thing which doth answer God's offer in the gospel, and maketh good our profession, as members of His church, it is a necessary duty lying upon us.

3. Whatsoever a man hath else, if he do not thus close with God's device concerning Christ Jesus, and do not receive Him, it doth not avail, either as to the accepting of his person, or of his performances, or as to the saving of his soul. Men are *accepted* only in Christ the Beloved – 'To the praise of the glory of His grace, wherein He hath made us accepted in the Beloved.' [*Eph* 1:6.] Abel and his offering are accepted by faith. 'Without faith it is impossible to please God' [*Heb* 11:4, 6]; and 'He that believeth not is condemned already, and shall not see life, but the wrath of God abideth on him.' [*John* 3:18, 36.] For want of this, no external title doth avail; the children of the kingdom are 'cast out,' if this be wanting. [*Matt* 8:10–12.] The people of Israel are like other heathens, in regard of a graceless state, lying open to the wrath of God – 'Behold, the days come, saith the Lord, that I will punish all them which are circumcised with the uncircumcised, Egypt and Judah, and Edom; for all these nations are uncircumcised, and all the house of Israel are uncircumcised in the heart.' [*Jer* 9:25, 26.] If men do not

believe that He who was slain at Jerusalem, who was called Christ Jesus, and witnessed unto by the prophets, and declared to be the Son of God by many mighty works – I say, if men do not believe that He is the way, and close not with Him as the only way, they shall die in their sins – 'I said therefore unto you, that ye shall die in your sins; for if ye believe not that I am He, ye shall die in your sins.' [*John* 8:24.]

We say, then, it is a most necessary duty thus to close with Christ Jesus, as the blessed relief appointed for sinners. Every one who is come to years of understanding, and heareth this gospel, is obliged to take to heart his own lost condition, and God's gracious offer of peace and salvation through Christ Jesus, and speedily to flee from the wrath to come, by accepting and closing with this offer, heartily acquiescing therein as a satisfying way for the salvation of perishing sinners. And, that all may be the more encouraged to set about this duty, when they hear Him praying them to be reconciled unto Him, let them remember that peace and salvation are offered in universal terms to all without exception: 'If any man will,' he shall be welcome. [*Rev* 22:17.] If any thirst, although after that which will never profit, yet they shall be welcome here, on the condition aforesaid – 'Ho, every one that thirsteth, come yet to the waters, and he that hath no money: come ye, buy and eat; yea, come, buy wine and milk, without money and without price. Wherefore do ye spend money for that which is not bread? and your labour for that which satisfieth not? hearken diligently unto me, and eat ye that which is good, and let your soul delight itself in fatness. Incline your ear, and come unto me: hear, and your soul shall live: and I will make an everlasting covenant with you, even the sure mercies of

David.' [*Is* 55:1–3.] All are 'commanded to believe.' This is His commandment, 'that we should believe on the name of His Son Jesus Christ.' [1 *John* 3:23.] The promises are to all who are externally called by the gospel. God excludes none, if they do not exclude themselves – 'The promise is unto you, and to your children, and to all that are afar off, even as many as the Lord our God shall call.' [*Acts* 2:39.] So that if any desire salvation, they may come forward, 'He will in no wise cast them out' [*John* 6:37], being 'able to save to the uttermost them that come unto God through Him.' [*Heb* 7:25.] And those who have long delayed to take this matter to heart, have now the more need to look to it, lest what belongs to their peace be hid from their eyes. But all these words will not take effect with people, until 'God pour out His Spirit from on high' [*Is* 32:15]; to cause them to approach unto God in Christ; yet we must still press men's duty upon them, and entreat and charge them by the appearing of the Lord Jesus Christ, and their reckoning to Him in that day, that they give the Lord no rest until He send out that 'Spirit, which He will give to them who ask it' [*Luke* 11:13], and cause them to know what belongs unto their peace, and bring them to their duty.

3 WHAT IS REQUIRED OF THOSE WHO WOULD BELIEVE ON CHRIST JESUS AND BE SAVED

We come now to speak of the *third* thing which is previously required of those who are to perform this duty. Men must not rashly, inconsiderately, and ignorantly, rush in upon this matter, saying, they approve of the device of saving sinners by Christ, and will acquiesce and rest on Him for safety. Often men do deceive themselves here, and do imagine that they have done the thing. We shall, therefore, notice some things pre-required in a person who is to close with Christ Jesus; which, although we offer not as positive qualifications, fitting a man for Christ that way: 'Come – without money, and without price' [*Is* 55:1]; yet they are such things as without them a man cannot knowingly and cordially perform the duty of believing on Christ Jesus.

Besides the common principles which are to be supposed in those who live under gospel-ordinances; as the knowledge that men have immortal souls; that soul and body will be united again at the last day; that there is a heaven and hell, one of which will be the everlasting portion of all men; that the Old and New Testaments are the true Word of God and the rule of faith and manners; that every man is by nature void of the grace of God, and is an enemy unto God, and an heir of condemnation; that reconciliation is only by the Mediator Christ Jesus; that faith unites unto Him, and is the condition of the new covenant; that holiness is the fruit of true faith, and is to be followed as that without which no man shall see God: I say, besides these things, the knowledge of which is necessary, it is required of him who would believe on Christ Jesus –

First, That he take to heart his natural condition; and here he must know some things, and be very serious about them; I say, he must know some things; as

1. That as he was born a rebel and an outlaw unto God, so he hath by many actual transgressions disobeyed God, and ratified the forfeiture of His favour: yea, a man should know many particular instances of his rebellion on all hands; as that he is a liar, Sabbath-breaker, blasphemer, or the like; as Paul speaketh very particularly of himself

afterwards – 'Who was before a blasphemer, and a persecutor, and injurious.' [1 *Tim* 1:13.]

2. The man must know that the wrath of God denounced in Scripture is standing in force against those very sins whereof he is guilty, and so, consequently, he is the party undoubtedly against whom God, who cannot lie, hath denounced war. A man must know, that when the Scripture saith, 'Cursed is he that offereth a corrupt thing unto God' [*Mal* 1:14]; it speaketh against him for his superficial service performed unto God with the outward man, when his heart was far off. When the word saith, 'The Lord will not hold him guiltless that taketh His name in vain' [*Exod* 20:7], the man must know it speaketh against himself, who hath often carelessly profaned that dreadful name, before which all knees shall bow [*Phil* 2:10]; and which His enemies do take in vain. [*Ps* 139:20.] When the word saith, 'Cursed is he that doeth the work of the Lord negligently' [*Jer* 48:10], the man must know that it speaks against himself, who hath irreverently, with much wandering of heart, and drowsiness, heard the word preached; and without sense, faith, or understanding, hath often prayed before Him. When the word saith, 'Woe be unto him that giveth his neighbour drink, and putteth his bottle to him, to make him drunk also' [*Hab* 2:15, 16], the man must know that it is spoken against himself, who hath gloried in making his neighbour drunk, and that dreadful wrath is determined by the Lord against him according to that scripture. When the word saith, 'God will judge unclean persons' [*Heb* 13:4], and will exclude them from the 'New Jerusalem, and they shall have their part in the lake which burneth with fire and brimstone' [*Rev* 21:8]; the man must know that the Scripture speaketh these very words against him, he being an unclean person;

so that he is the person against whom the curses of the law do directly strike.

3. A man must know that he hath nothing of his own to procure his peace, and to set him free from the hazard under which he lieth; because 'all his righteousness is as an unclean thing.' [*Is* 64:6.] His prayers, his other services done to God, his alms-deeds, etc., are not acceptable unto God, since they came not from a right principle in his heart, and were not performed in a right way, nor upon a right account, nor for a right end; his 'sacrifices have been an abomination unto God.' [*Prov* 21:27.]

4. He must know, that as he is void of all the saving graces of the Spirit, as the true love of God, the true fear of His name, godly sorrow for sin, etc., so particularly, that he wants faith in Christ, who taketh away the sins of all them who believe on Him. Until a man know this, he will still leave all his debt and burden, without care or regard anywhere else, before he bring it to the Surety.

Now, not only must a man know these things, as I said before, but he must also very seriously take them to heart; that is to say, he must be affected with these things, and must be in earnest about them, as he used to be in other cases in which he is most serious; yea, he should be more in earnest here than in other cases, because it is of greater concernment unto him. This seriousness produceth –

1. A taking of salvation to heart more than anything else. Shall men be obliged to 'seek first the kingdom of God? [*Matt* 6:33]; is there but 'one thing necessary?' [*Luke* 10:42]; shall Paul 'count all things loss and dung' for this matter [*Phil* 3:8]; is a man a loser, if he gain 'the whole world and lose his own soul?' [*Mark* 8:36]; shall this be the only ground of joy, 'that men's names are written in the book of life?' [*Luke* 10:20]; and shall not

men, who would be reckoned serious, take their soul and salvation more to heart than anything else? Surely it cannot fail. Let none deceive themselves. If the hazard of their soul, and the salvation thereof, and how to be in favour with God, have not gone nearer to their heart than anything in the world beside, it cannot be presumed, upon just grounds, that they have known sin, or God, or the eternity of His wrath, aright.

2. This seriousness breaks the man's heart, and causeth the stoutness of it to faint, and leadeth it out to sorrow as for a first-born. [*Zech* 12:10.] I grant their sorrow will better suit that scripture afterwards, when they apprehend Christ pierced by their sins.

3. It leads the man to a self-loathing. A man taking up himself so, cannot but loathe himself for his abominations, whereby he hath destroyed himself. There is somewhat of that spirit of revenge, which is mentioned as a fruit of true repentance – 'This self-same thing that ye sorrowed after a godly sort, what carefulness it wrought in you; yea, what revenge!' [2 *Cor* 7:11.]

4. This seriousness makes the man peremptory to find relief; since it is not in himself. He dare not put off and delay his business as before; and this is indeed required, that he finds himself so pursued and urged to it, that he flees for refuge somewhere. I grant some have a higher and some a lesser degree of this seriousness, as we showed in the former part of this treatise: but if we speak of the Lord's ordinary way of working with those who are come to age, we say, they must very seriously take their soul's estate to heart, despairing of help in themselves, since 'the whole need not a physician, but those who are sick.' [*Matt* 9:12.] As for the measure, we plead only that which probably supposes that a man will be induced thereby to

treat cordially with Christ, on any terms he doth offer Himself to be closed with.

The *second* thing pre-required of him who would believe on Christ Jesus is, He must know and take to heart the way of escape from God's wrath; the Spirit must convince him of that righteousness. Here a man must understand somewhat distinctly, that God hath devised a way to save poor lost man by Jesus Christ, whose perfect righteousness hath satisfied offended justice, and procured pardon and everlasting favour to all those whom He persuadeth, by this gospel, to accept of God's offer – 'Be it known unto you, therefore, that through this man is preached unto you the forgiveness of sins; and by Him all that believe are justified from all things.' [*Acts* 13:38, 39.] 'As many as received Him, to them gave He power to become the sons of God, even to them that believe on His name.' [*John* 1:12.] So that no person is excluded, of whatsoever rank or condition, whatsoever hath been his former way, unless he be guilty of the sin against the Holy Ghost, which is a malicious hatred and rejection of the remedy appointed for sinners, as we shall hear; for 'all manner of sins' are forgiven unto those who accept of the offer in God's way. [*Matt* 12:31.] 'He is able to save to the uttermost them that come unto God through Him.' [*Heb* 7:25.]

The *third* thing pre-required is, A man must know, that as God hath not excluded him from the relief appointed, so He is willing to be reconciled unto men through Christ, and hath obliged men to close with Him through Christ Jesus, and so to appropriate that salvation to themselves. He not only invites all to come – 'Ho, every one that thirsteth, come ye to the waters, and he that hath no money: come ye, buy and eat; yea, come, buy wine and milk, without money and without price' [*Is*

55:1, 2]; and welcometh all that come, as we find in the gospel, and commendeth those who come, as the centurion and the woman of Canaan [*Matt* 8:10; 15:28]; and chideth for not coming and closing with Him, 'Ye will not come to Me, that ye might have life' [*John* 5:40]; and condemneth for not closing so with Him: 'He that believeth not is condemned already' [*John* 3:18]; but He also commandeth all to believe on Christ: 'This is His commandment, that we should believe on the name of His Son Jesus Christ.' [1 *John* 3:23.] So that a man is not to question the Lord's willingness to receive men who go to Christ honestly, for God hath abundantly cleared that in Scripture. Unless a man know so much, he will scarcely dare to lay his heart open for that noble plan of saving sinners, or adventure the whole weight of his salvation upon Christ Jesus.

The *fourth* thing pre-required is, The man who would close with Christ Jesus, must resolve to break all covenants with hell and death – 'Because ye have said, we have made a covenant with death, and with hell are we at agreement; when the overflowing scourge shall pass through, it shall not come unto us; for we have made lies our refuge, and under falsehood have we hid ourselves.' [*Is* 28:15.] Whatsoever known evil men are engaged in, they must resolve to forego it; for there is no concord between Christ and Belial. [2 *Cor* 6:14–18.] The Lord requireth that they who would expect 'Him to be for them, should not be for another.' [*Hos* 3:3.] This is far from evangelical repentance, which I grant doth not precede a man's closing with Christ by faith: there is little here beyond a disregard of those things into which a man was formerly devoted, and a slighting what he was mad upon, because he seeth himself destroyed thereby, and relief now offered; upon which his heart beginneth to be more intent than formerly it was. After this when Christ is looked upon alone, His worth and beauty do appear, so as among all the gods there is none like unto Him, and He appeareth as a sufficient covering of the eyes to all who obtain Him: upon which the heart loves God's plan in the new covenant, and desires to lay its weight upon Christ rather than any other way, bending towards Him; and so the man becomes a believer.

Now, I will not say that all these things, whereof we have spoken, are formally, orderly, and distinctly found in every person before he close with God in Christ; for the way of the heart with Christ may be added to 'the four wonderful things.' [*Prov* 30:18.] It is hard to trace the heart in its translation from darkness to light, yet we hold out the most ordinary and likely way to him who doth ask the way; debarring thereby ignorant and senseless persons from meddling, and discharging them from pretending to any interest in Him whilst they remain such.

4 WHAT IS INVOLVED IN THE DUTY, TOGETHER WITH ITS VARIOUS ASPECTS

The *fourth* thing we proposed to speak to is, The properties of this duty, when rightly gone about. I shall only mention a few.

1. Believing on Christ must be personal; a man himself and in his own proper person must close with Christ Jesus – 'The just shall live by his faith.' [*Hab* 2:4.] This saith, that it will not suffice for a man's safety and relief, that he is in covenant with God as a born member of the visible church, by virtue of the parent's subjection to God's ordinances: neither will it suffice that the person had the

initiating seal of baptism added, and that he then virtually engaged to seek salvation by Christ's blood, as all infants do: neither doth it suffice that men are come of believing parents; their faith will not instate their children into a right to the spiritual blessings of the covenant; neither will it suffice that parents did, in some respects, engage for their children, and give them away unto God: all these things do not avail. The children of the kingdom and of godly predecessors are cast out. Unless a man in his own person have faith in Christ Jesus, and with his own heart approve, and acquiesce in that device of saving sinners, he cannot be saved. I grant, this faith is given unto him by Christ; but certain it is, that it must be personal.

Secondly, This duty must be *cordial* and *hearty* – 'With the heart man believeth unto righteousness.' [*Rom* 10:10.] A man must be sincere, and without guile, in closing with Christ, judging Him the only covering of the eyes, not hankering after another way. The matter must not swim only in the head or understanding, but it must be in the heart: the man must not only be persuaded that Christ is the way, but affectionately persuaded of it, loving and liking the thing, having complacency in it; so that 'it is all a man's desire,' as David speaketh of the covenant. [2 *Sam* 23:5.] If a man be cordial and affectionate in anything, surely he must be so here in this 'one thing that is necessary.' It must not be simply a fancy in the head, it must be a heart-business, a soul-business; yea, not a business in the outer court of the affections, but in the flower of the affections, and in the innermost cabinet of the soul, where Christ is formed. Shall a man be cordial in anything, and not in this, which comprises all his chief interests and his everlasting state within it? Shall the Lord be said to 'rejoice over a man as a bridegroom rejoiceth over his bride?' [*Is* 62:5]; and 'to rest in His love with joy?' [*Zeph* 3:17]; and shall not the heart of man go out and meet Him here? The heart or nothing; love or nothing; marriage-love, which goeth from heart to heart; love of espousals, or nothing – 'My son, give me thine heart.' [*Prov* 23:26.] 'Though I bestow all my goods to feed the poor and though I give my body to be burned, and have not charity, it profiteth me nothing.' [1 *Cor* 13:2.] I will not say that there is in all, as soon as they believe, a prevailing sensible love, which maketh sick; but there must be in believing, a rational and kindly love, so well grounded and deeply engaged, that 'many waters cannot quench it. It is strong as death, and jealousy in it burneth as fire.' [*Cant* 8:6, 7.]

3. The third property or qualification of believing, as it goeth out after Christ, is that it must be *rational*. By this I mean that the man should move towards God in Christ, in knowledge and understanding, taking up God's device of saving sinners by Christ as the Scripture holds it out; not fancying a Christ to himself otherwise than the gospel speaketh of Him, nor another way of relief by Him than the word of God holdeth out. Therefore we find *knowledge* joined to the covenant between God and man as a requisite – 'And I will give them a heart to know Me, that I am the Lord; and they shall be my people, and I will be their God.' 'And they shall teach no more every man his neighbour, and every man his brother, saying, Know the Lord: for they shall all know Me, from the least of them unto the greatest of them, saith the Lord.' [*Jer* 24:7; 31:34.] I mean also, that a man must be in calmness of spirit, and as it were in his cold blood, in closing with Christ Jesus; not in a simple fit of affection, which soon vanisheth – 'He that received the seed into stony places,

the same is he that heareth the word, and anon with joy receiveth it' [*Matt* 13:20]; nor in a distemper through some outward distress, as the people were, 'when He slew them, then they sought Him; and proved not steadfast in the covenant' [*Ps* 78:34]; nor under a temptation of some outward temporary interest, as Simon Magus was when he believed. A man must act here rationally, as being master of himself, in some measure able to judge of the good or evil of the thing as it stands before him.

4. The *fourth* is faith; as it goeth out rationally, so it goeth out *resolutely*. The poor distressed people in the gospel did most resolutely cast themselves upon Christ. This resoluteness of spirit is in respect to all difficulties that lie in the way; violence is offered to these. The man whose heart is a laying out for Christ Jesus, cannot say, 'There is a lion in the street.' [*Prov* 26:13.] If he cannot have access by the door, he will break through the roof of the house. [*Luke* 5:19.] He often does not regard that which the world calls *discretion* or *prudence*, like Zaccheus, climbing up on a tree to see Christ, when faith was forming in his bosom. [*Luke* 19.] This resoluteness of spirit foresees what inconveniences may follow, and disregards all these; at least resolving over all these, like a wise builder who reckoneth the expense beforehand. [*Luke* 14:28.] This resoluteness is also in regard to all a man's idols, and such weights as would easily beset him, if he did not follow after Christ over them all, like that blind man who did cast his garment from him when Christ called him. [*Mark* 10:50.] This resoluteness in the soul proceedeth from desperate self-necessity within the man, as it was with the jailer [*Acts* 16:30]; and from the sovereign command of God, obliging the man to move towards Christ – 'This is His commandment, that we should believe on the

name of His Son Jesus Christ' [1 *John* 3:23]; and from the good report gone abroad of God, that 'He putteth none away that come unto Him through Christ' [*John* 6:37]; but commends such as do adventure over the greatest difficulties, as the woman of Canaan. [*Matt* 15:28.] But, above all, this resoluteness doth proceed from the arm of JEHOVAH, secretly and strongly drawing the sinner towards Christ – 'No man can come to Me, except the Father, which hath sent Me, draw him.' [*John* 6:44.]

I will not say that every one, closing with Christ in the offers of the gospel, hath all the above thoughts formally in his mind; yet, upon search, it will be found, if he be put to it, or put in mind of these things, they are then uppermost in the soul.

By what is said, it manifestly appears that many in the visible church had need to do somewhat further for securing of their soul, when they come to years of discretion, than is found to have been done by them before, in the covenant between God and the church, sealed to them in baptism.

From what is said also, there is a competent guard upon the free grace of God in the gospel, held out through Christ Jesus; so that ignorant, senseless, profane men, cannot with any shadow of reason, pretend to an interest in it. It is true, believing in Christ, and closing with Him as a perfect Saviour, seemeth easy, and every godless man saith that he believes on Him: but they deceive themselves, since their soul hath never cordially, rationally, and resolutely gone out after Christ Jesus, as we have said. It may be, some wicked men have been *enlightened* [*Heb* 6:4]; and have found some reality in their fear – 'Felix trembled' [*Acts* 24:25]; or in their joy – 'He that received the seed into stony places, the same is he that heareth the word, and anon with joy receiveth it' [*Matt* 13:20]; and Herod heard John 'gladly' [*Mark* 6:20]; but not having engaged their heart in approaching to God [*Jer* 30:21], have either sat down in that common work, as their sanctuary, until the trial came – 'When tribulation or persecution ariseth because of the word, by and by he is offended' [*Matt* 13:21]; or, 'they return back with the dog to their vomit,' from which they had in some measure 'escaped by the knowledge of the Lord and Saviour' [2 *Peter* 2:20–22]; or they utterly fall away to the hatred and malicious despising and persecuting of Christ and His interests, from whence hardly can they be recovered – 'For it is impossible for those who were once enlightened, and have tasted of the heavenly gift, and were made partakers of the Holy Ghost, and have tasted the good word of God, and the powers of the world to come, if they shall fall away, to renew them again unto repentance; seeing they crucify to themselves the Son of God afresh, and put Him to an open shame.' 'For if we sin wilfully after that we have received the knowledge of the truth, there remaineth no more sacrifice for sins.' Of how much sorer punishment, suppose ye, shall he be thought worthy, who hath trodden under foot the Son of God, and hath counted the blood of the covenant, wherewith he was sanctified, an unholy thing, and hath done despite unto the Spirit of grace?' [*Heb* 6:4–6; 10:26–29.] Which things should provoke men to be serious in this great business.

5 THE EFFECTS AND OUTCOMES OF SAVING FAITH

We come now to speak to the *fifth* thing proposed, and that is, What are the native consequences of true believing? I shall reduce what I have to speak of them to these two, namely, union with God, and communion. *First*, then, I say, When a sinner closeth with Christ Jesus, there is presently an admirable union, a strange oneness between God and the man. As the husband and wife, head and body, root and branches, are not to be reckoned two but one; so Christ, or God in Christ, and the sinner closing with Him by faith, are one – 'We are members of His body, of His flesh, and of His bones.' [*Eph* 5:30.] He that is so 'joined unto the Lord is one spirit' [1 *Cor* 6:17]; as the Father is in the Son, and Christ in the Father, so believers are one in the Father and the Son; they are one, as the Father and Son are one. The Father in Christ, and Christ in believers, that they may be 'made perfect in one.' O what a strange interweaving and indissoluble union here! [*John* 17:21–26.]

Because of this union betwixt God and the believer 1. They can never hate one another. Henceforth the Lord will never hate the believer – 'As no man hateth his own flesh at any time, but cherisheth and nourisheth it,' so doth Christ His people. [*Eph* 5:29.] He may be angry, so as to correct and chastise the man that is a believer; but all He doth to him is for his good and advantage – 'All the Lord's paths must be mercy and truth to him.' [*Ps* 25:10.] 'All things work together for good to him.' [*Rom* 8:28.] On the other side, the believer can never hate God maliciously; for – 'He that is born of God sinneth not.' [1 *John* 3:9.] For the Lord hath resolved and ordained things so, that His hand shall undoubtedly so be upon all believers for good, that they shall never be permitted to hate Him, and so be plucked out of His hand.

2. Because of this union there is a strange sympathy and fellow-feeling between God and the believer: the

Lord is afflicted with the man's affliction. [*Is* 63:9.] He doth tenderly, carefully, and seasonably resent it, as if He were afflicted with it. He who toucheth the believer, toucheth the apple of the Lord's eye [*Zech* 2:8] – 'He is touched with the feeling of their infirmities' [*Heb* 4:15]; and 'precious in His sight is their death.' [*Ps* 116:15.] In a word, what is done to them, is done unto Him; and what is not done unto them, is not done unto Him – 'He that receiveth you, receiveth Me.' [*Matt* 10:40.] 'Inasmuch as ye have done it unto one of the least of these My brethren, ye have done it unto Me: inasmuch as ye did it not to one of the least of these, ye did it not to Me.' [*Matt* 25:40, 45.] On the other part, the 'zeal of His house' occupieth the heart of the believer. [*Ps* 69:9.] 'The Lord's reproach' lighteth on the believer. If it go well with His affairs, that is the business of His people. So there is a strange sympathy between God and believers, all by virtue of the union between them; because of which, men should hate everything which would compete with Him in their love or affections, and should disdain to be slaves to the creatures, since these are the servants of their Lord and husband, and their servants through Him. What a hateful thing for a queen to disgrace herself with the servants of her prince and husband! It is also a shame for a believer to be 'afraid of evil tidings,' since the Lord, with whom he is one, alone ruleth all things, 'and doth whatsoever pleaseth Him in heaven and earth.' 'All things are yours, and ye are Christ's, and Christ is God's.' Surely he shall not be moved for ever, he shall not be afraid of evil tidings; his heart is fixed, trusting in the Lord; his heart is established, he shall not be afraid.' 'Our God is in the heavens, He hath done whatsoever He pleased.' [1 *Cor* 3:21, 23; *Ps* 112:6, 7; 115:3.]

The other great consequence of believing, is an admirable unparalleled *communion*, by virtue whereof 1. The parties themselves do belong each to the other. The Lord is the God of His people; He Himself, Father, Son, and Holy Ghost, is their God, in all His glorious attributes; His justice as well as His mercy; His wisdom, power, holiness, etc., for He becomes the God of His people, as He often speaks in the covenant. On the other part, believers are His people. In their very persons they are His, as the covenant doth speak; they shall be His people; their head, their heart, their hand, etc.; whatsoever they are, they are His.

2. By virtue of this communion they have a mutual interest in one another's whole goods and property, so far as can be useful. All the Lord's word belongs to the believer; threatenings as well as promises are for his good; all His ways, all His works of all sorts, special communications, death, devils, even all things so far as can be useful – 'All things are yours; whether Paul, or Apollos, or Cephas, or the world, or life, or death, or things present, or things to come; all are yours, and ye are Christ's, and Christ is God's.' [1 *Cor* 3:21–23.] On the other side, all that belongs to the believer is the Lord's; heritage, children, life, wife, credit, etc., all is at His disposing; if any of these can be useful to Him, the believer is to forego them, else he falsifies that communion, and declares himself in so far unworthy of Christ. 'If any man come to me, and hate not his father; yea, and his own life also, he cannot be my disciple.' [*Luke* 14:26.]

3. By virtue of this communion, there should be much intimacy and familiarity between God and the believer. The Lord may interfere with any thing which belongs to

the believer, and do unto him what seemeth good to Him; and the man is not to mistake, or say unto God, 'What doest Thou?' except in so far as concerns His duty: yea, He is still to say, in every case, 'Good is the word and will of the Lord.' [*Is* 39:8; 2 *Kings* 4:23, 26.] On the other part, the believer may, in a humble way, be homely and familiar with God in Christ; He may come with 'boldness to the throne of grace' [*Heb* 4:16]; and present his addresses unto God. He is no more a stranger unto God, so that he needs not speak unto God as one who has acquaintances to make every hour, as many professors do; which makes a great inconsistency in their religion.

The believer also may lay open all his heart unto God – 'I have poured out my soul before the Lord' [1 *Sam* 1:15]; and impart all his secrets unto Him, and all his temptations, without fear of a mistake. The believer also may inquire into what God doth, in so far as may concern his own duty, or in so far as may ward off mistakes respecting the Lord's way, and reconcile it with His words: so Job says, 'Though He slay me, yet will I trust in Him; but I will maintain mine own ways before Him.' [*Job* 13:15.] The believer is a friend in this respect, as 'knowing what the Master doeth'; see *Gen* 18:23; *Jer* 12:1; *Is* 63:17.

The believer also may draw near daily unto God with all his failings, and seek repentance, pardon, and peace, through the advocacy of Christ – 'Him hath God exalted with His right hand, to be a Prince and a Saviour, to give repentance to Israel and forgiveness of sins.' [*Acts* 5:31.] 'If any man sin, we have an advocate with the Father, Jesus Christ the righteous.' [1 *John* 2:1.] O how often in one day may the believer plead pardon, if he intend not to mock God, nor turn His grace into licentiousness! The Lord hath commanded men to forgive seventy times seven in one day; and has intimated there, in a parable of a king who took account of his servants, how much more the Master will forgive. [*Matt* 18:22–27.]

The believer also may intrust God with all His outward concerns, for He careth for these things – 'If God so clothe the grass of the field, shall He not much more clothe you, O ye of little faith? Therefore, take no thought, saying, What shall we eat, or What shall we drink, or, Wherewithal shall we be clothed? for your heavenly Father knoweth that ye have need of all these things.' [*Matt* 6:30–32.] 'Casting all your care upon Him, for He careth for you.' [1 *Peter* 5:7.] Yea, the believer may humbly put God to it to make Him forthcoming to him in all such cases as beseemeth, and to help him to suitable fruit in every season, 'even grace in time of need.' [*Heb* 4:16.] Yea, how great things may believers seek from him in Christ Jesus, both for themselves and others! 'If we ask anything according to His will, He heareth us.' [1 *John* 5:14, 15.] 'Whatsoever ye shall ask in my name, that will I do.' [*John* 14:13.] 'Ask of me things to come concerning my sons: and concerning the work of my hands, command ye me.' [*Is* 45:11.] It is the shame and great prejudice of His people that they do not improve that communion with God more than they do: Christ may justly upbraid them, 'that they ask nothing in His name.' [*John* 16:24.]

By what is said, it appears of how great consequence this duty of believing is, by which a man closes with Christ Jesus, whom the Father hath sealed and given for a covenant to the people. It is so honourable to God, answering His very design, and serving His interest in the whole contrivance and manifestation of the gospel; and it is so advantageous to men, that Satan and an evil heart of unbelief do mightily oppose it, by moving objections against it, of which I shall notice the most ordinary.

CHAPTER III

Objections and difficulties explained and answered

I THE SINNER'S BASENESS RENDERING IT PRESUMPTION TO COME TO CHRIST

Objection: I am so base, worthless, and weak of myself that I think it were high presumption for me to meddle with Christ Jesus, or the salvation purchased at the price of His blood.

Answer: It is true, all the children of Adam are base and wicked before Him, 'who chargeth His angels with folly [*Job* 4:18.] 'All nations are less than nothing and vanity before him.' [*Is* 40:17.] There is such a disproportion between God and man, that unless He Himself had devised that covenant, and of His own free will had offered so to transact with men, it had been high treason for men or angels to have imagined that God should have humbled Himself, and become a servant, and have taken on Him our nature, and have united it by a personal union to the blessed Godhead; and that He should have subjected Himself to the shameful death of the cross; and all this, that men, who were rebels, should be reconciled unto God, and be made eternally happy, by being in His holy company for ever.

But I say, all this was His own device and free choice; yea, moreover, if God had not sovereignly commanded men so to close with Him in and through Christ, no man durst have made use of that device of His – 'Ho, every one that thirsteth, come ye to the waters, and he that hath no money: come ye, buy and eat; yea, come, buy wine and milk without money and without price.' [*Is* 55:1–3.] 'And this is His commandment, that we should believe on the name of His son Jesus Christ.' [1 *John* 3:23.] So then, although with Abigail I may say, 'Let me be but a servant, to wash the feet of the servants of my Lord' [1 *Sam* 25:41]; yet, since He hath in His holy wisdom devised that way, and knows how to be richly glorified in it – 'The eyes of your understanding being enlightened, that ye may know, what is the riches of the glory of His inheritance in the saints' [*Eph* 1:18]; 'All Mine are Thine, and Thine are Mine, and I am glorified in them' [*John* 17:10]; and hath commanded me, as I shall be answerable at the great day, to close with Him in Christ, I dare not disobey, nor inquire into the reasons of His contrivance and commands, but must comply with the command, as I would not be found to 'frustrate the grace of God' [*Gal* 2:21]; and in a manner disappoint the gospel, and falsify the record which God hath borne of His Son, 'that there is life enough in Him for men' [1 *John* 5:10, 11], and so 'make God a liar,' and add that rebellion to all my former transgressions.

2 THE SINGULARITY OF HIS SIN BARRING THE WAY

Objection: I am a person singularly sinful, beyond any I know: therefore I dare not presume to go near to Christ Jesus, or look after that salvation which is through His righteousness.

Answer: Is your sin beyond the drunkenness and incest of Lot; adultery covered with murder in David; idolatry and horrid apostasy in Solomon; idolatry, murder, and witchcraft in Manasseh; anger against God and His way in Jonah; forswearing of Christ in Peter, after he was forewarned, and had vowed the contrary; bloody persecution in Paul, making the saints to blaspheme? etc. But woe to him who is emboldened to sin by these instances recorded in Scripture, and adduced here to the commendation of the free and rich grace of God, and to encourage poor penitent sinners to flee unto Christ; I say, are your sins beyond these? yet all these obtained pardon through Christ, as the Scripture showeth.

Know, therefore, that all sins are equal before the free grace of God, 'who loveth freely' [*Hos* 14:4]; and looketh not to less or more sin. If the person have a heart to 'come unto Him through Christ, then He is able to save to the uttermost.' [*Heb* 7:25.] Yea, it is more provoking before God, not to close with Christ, when the offer comes to a man, than all the rest of his transgressions are; for 'he, that believeth not hath made God a liar,' in that record He hath borne of life in the Son. [1 *John* 5:10, 11.] 'And he who doth not believe, shall be condemned for not believing on the Son of God.' [*John* 3:18.] That shall be the main thing in his indictment; so that much sin cannot excuse a man, if he reject Christ, and refuse His offer; since God hath openly declared, that 'this is a faithful saying, and worthy of all acceptation, that Christ Jesus came to save sinners, whereof I am chief.' Even he who is *chief* of sinners in his own apprehension, is bound to believe and 'accept this saying.' [1 *Tim* 1:15.]

3 SPECIAL AGGRAVATIONS OF SIN A HINDRANCE

Objection: My sins have some aggravating circumstances beyond the same sins in other persons, which doth much terrify me.

Answer: What can the aggravations of thy sins be, which are not paralleled in the foregoing examples? Is thy sin against great light? so were many of those of whom we spake before. Was it against singular mercies and deliverances? so was that of Lot's and Noah's drunkenness. Was thy sin done with much deliberation? so was David's, when he wrote the letter against Uriah. Was it against or after any singular manifestation of God? so was Solomon's. Was it by a small and despicable temptation? so was that of Jonah and of Peter, if we consider the heinousness of their transgressions. Hast thou reiterated the sin, and committed it over again? so did Lot, so did Peter, so did Jehoshaphat, in joining with Ahab and Jehoram. [1 *Kings* 22; 2 *Kings* 3.] Are there many gross sins concurring together in thee? So were there in Manasseh. Hast thou stood long out in rebellion? that, as all the former, is thy shame; but so did the thief on the cross; he stood it out to the last gasp. [*Luke* 23:42, 43.] If yet 'thou hast an ear to hear,' thou art commanded 'to hear.' [*Matt* 13:9.] Although thou hast long 'spent thy money for that which is not bread' [*Is* 55:1, 3], thou hast the greater need now to make haste and to flee for refuge; and if thou do so, He shall welcome thee, and 'in no wise cast thee out' [*John* 6:37]; especially, since He hath used no prescription of time in Scripture. So that all those aggravations of thy sin, will not excuse thy refusing the Lord's offer.

4 SINS NOT NAMED ARE A BARRIER

Objection: In all those instances given, you have not named the particulars of which I am guilty; nor know I any who ever obtained mercy before God, being guilty of such things as are in me.

Answer: It is difficult to notice every particular transgression which may vex the conscience; yea, lesser sins than some of those I have mentioned may very much disquiet, if the Lord awaken the conscience. But, for thy satisfaction, I shall refer to some truths of Scripture, which do reach sins and cases more universally than any man can do particularly: *Exod* 34:7 – 'God pardoneth iniquity, transgression, and sin'; that is, all manner of sin. If a man turn from all his wickedness, it shall no more be remembered, or prove his ruin. [*Ezek* 18:21, 22, 30.] 'Him that cometh He will in nowise cast out' [*John* 6:37]; that is, whatsoever be his sins, or the aggravations of them. 'Whosoever believeth shall have everlasting life' [*John* 3:16]; that is, without exception of any sin or any case. 'He is able to save to the uttermost those who come to God through Him' [*Heb* 7:25]; no man can sufficiently declare what is God's *uttermost*. 'All manner of sin and blasphemy shall be forgiven unto men' [*Matt* 12:31]; that is, there is no sort of sin, whereof one instance shall not be forgiven in one person or other, 'except the sin against the Holy Ghost.' These and the like scriptures carry all sorts of sin before them: so that let thy sins be what they will, or can be, they may be sunk in one of these truths; so that thy sin can be no excuse to thee for refusing the offers of peace and salvation through Christ, since 'any man who will,' is allowed to 'come and take.' [*Rev* 22:17.]

We will not multiply words: the great God of heaven and earth hath sovereignly commanded all who see their need of relief to betake themselves unto Christ Jesus, and to close cordially with God's device of saving sinners by Him, laying aside all objections and excuses, as they shall be answerable unto Him in the day when He shall judge the quick and the dead; and shall drive away from His presence all those who would dare to say, their sins and condition were such as that they durst not adventure upon Christ's perfect righteousness for their relief, notwithstanding of the Lord's own command often interposed, and, in a manner, His credit engaged.

5 THE SIN AGAINST THE HOLY GHOST ALLEGED

Objection: I suspect I am guilty of the 'sin against the Holy Ghost,' and so am incapable of pardon; and therefore I need not think of believing on Christ Jesus for the saving of my soul.

Answer: Although none should charge this sin on themselves, or on others, unless they can prove and establish the charge according to Christ's example – 'And whosoever speaketh a word against the Son of man, it shall be forgiven him: but whosoever speaketh against the Holy Ghost, it shall not be forgiven him, neither in this world, neither in the world to come' [*Matt* 12:31, 32]: yet for satisfying of the doubt, I shall (1) Show what is not the sin against the Holy Ghost, properly so called, because there be some gross sins which people do unwarrantably judge to be this unpardonable sin. (2) I shall show what is the sin against the Holy Ghost. (3) I shall draw some conclusions in answer directly to the objection.

[1] *What it is not*

As for the *first*, There be many gross sins, which although, as all other sins, they be sins against the Holy Ghost, who is God equal and one with the Father and the Son, and are done against some of His operations and motions; yet are they not that sin against the Holy Ghost which is the unpardonable sin. As, (1) Blaspheming of God under bodily tortures is not that sin; for some saints fell into this sin – 'And I punished them oft in every synagogue, and compelled them to blaspheme' [*Acts* 26:11]; much less blaspheming of God in a fit of distraction or frenzy; for a man is not a free rational agent at that time; and 'He that spareth His people, as a father doth the son that serveth him, and pitieth them that fear Him, as a father pitieth his children' [*Mal* 3:17; *Ps* 103:13]; so doth He spare and pity in these rovings; for so would our fathers according to the flesh do, if we blasphemed them in a fit of distraction. Much less are horrid blasphemies against God darted in upon the soul, and not allowed there, this unpardonable sin; for such things were offered to Christ, and are often cast in upon the saints. [*Matt* 4:1–11.]

2. The hating of good in others, whilst I am not convinced that it is good, but according to my light, judge it to be evil; yea, the speaking against it, yea, the persecuting of it in that case, is not the sin against the Holy Ghost; for all these will be found in Paul before he was converted; and he obtained mercy because he did these things ignorantly.

3. Heart-rising at the thriving of others in the work and way of God, whilst I love it in myself; yea, the rising of the heart against Providence, which often expresses itself against the creatures nearest our hand; yea, this rising of heart entertained and maintained (although they be horrid things leading towards that unpardonable sin, yet) are not that sin; for these may be in the saints proceeding from self-love, which cannot endure to be darkened by another, and proceeding from some cross in their idol under a fit of temptation: the most part of all this was in Jonah (chapter 4).

4. Not only are not decays in what once was in the man, and falling into gross sins against light after the receiving of the truth, this unpardonable sin; for then many of the saints in Scripture were undone; but further, apostasy from much of the truth is not that sin; for that was in Solomon, and in the churches of Corinth and Galatia; yea, denying, yea, forswearing of the most fundamental truth, under a great temptation, is not this sin: for then Peter had been undone.

5. As resisting, quenching, grieving, and vexing of the Spirit of God by many sinful ways, are not this unpardonable sin; for they are charged with those who are called to repentance in Scripture, and not shut out as guilty of this sin: so neither reiterated sin against light is the sin against the Holy Ghost, although it leads towards it, for such was Peter's sin in denying Christ; so was Jehoshaphat's sin in joining with Ahab and Jehoram.

6. Purposes and attempts of self-murder, and even purposes of murdering godly men, the party being under a sad fit of temptation; yea, actual self-murder (although probably it is often joined in the issue with this unpardonable sin, which ought to make every soul look upon the very temptation to it with horror and abhorrence, yet) is not the sin against the Holy Ghost. The jailer intended to kill himself upon a worse account than many poor people do, in the sight and sense of God's wrath, and of their own sin and corruption; yet that jailer obtained pardon [*Acts* 16:27, 34]; and Paul, before his effectual calling, was accessory unto the murder of many saints, and intended to kill more, as himself granteth – 'I verily thought with myself that I ought to do many things contrary to the name of Jesus of Nazareth. Which thing I also did in Jerusalem: and many of the saints did I shut

up in prison, having received authority from the chief priests; and when they were put to death, I gave my voice against them. And I punished them oft in every synagogue, and compelled them to blaspheme: and, being exceedingly mad against them, I persecuted them even unto strange cities.' [*Acts* 26:9–11.]

Although all these are dreadful sins, each of them deserving wrath everlasting, and, not being repented of, bringing endless vengeance; especially the last cuts off hope of relief, for anything that can be expected in an ordinary way; yet none of these is the unpardonable sin against the Holy Ghost: and so under any of these there is hope to him that hath an ear to hear the joyful sound of the covenant. All manner of such sin and blasphemy may be forgiven, as is clear in the Scripture, where these things are mentioned.

[2] *What it is*

As for the *second* thing: Let us see what the sin against the Holy Ghost is. It is not a simple act of transgression, but a combination of many mischievous things, involving soul and body ordinarily in guilt. We thus describe it – It is a rejecting and opposing of the chief gospel truth, and way of salvation, made out particularly to a man by the Spirit of God, in the truth and good thereof; and that avowedly, freely, wilfully, maliciously, and despitefully, working hopeless fear. There be three places of Scripture which do speak most of this sin, and thence we will prove every part of this description, in so far as may be useful to our present purpose; by which it will appear, that none who have a mind for Christ need stumble at what is spoken of this sin in Scripture – 'Wherefore I say unto you, All manner of sin and blasphemy shall be forgiven unto men: but the blasphemy against the Holy Ghost shall not be forgiven unto men. And whosoever speaketh a word against the Son of man, it shall be forgiven him: but whosoever speaketh against the Holy Ghost, it shall not be forgiven him, neither in this world, neither in the world to come.' 'For it is impossible for those who were once enlightened, and have tasted of the heavenly gift, and were made partakers of the Holy Ghost, and have tasted the good word of God, and the powers of the world to come, if they shall fall away, to renew them again unto repentance: seeing they crucify to themselves the Son of God afresh, and put Him to an open shame.' 'For if we sin wilfully after that we have received the knowledge of the truth, there remaineth no more sacrifice for sins, but a certain fearful looking for of judgment and fiery indignation, which shall devour the adversaries. He that despised Moses' law died without mercy under two or three witnesses: of how much sorer punishment, suppose ye, shall he be thought worthy, who hath trodden under foot the Son of God, and hath counted the blood of the covenant wherewith He was sanctified, an unholy thing, and hath done despite unto the Spirit of grace?' [*Matt* 12:23–32; *Heb* 6:4–6; 10:25–29.]

1. Then let us consider the object about which this sin, or sinful acting of the man guilty thereof, is conversant, and that is the chief gospel-truth and way of salvation; both which come to one thing. It is the way which God hath contrived for saving of sinners by Jesus Christ, the promised Messiah and Saviour, by whose death and righteousness men are to be saved, as He hath held Him forth in the ordinances, confirming the same by many mighty works in Scripture tending thereto. This way of salvation is the object. The Pharisees oppose this that

Christ was the Messiah – 'And all the people said, Is not this the son of David? But when the Pharisees heard it, they said, This fellow doth not cast out devils, but by Beelzebub the prince of the devils.' [*Matt* 12:23, 24.] The wrong is done against the Son of God – 'It is impossible to renew them again unto repentance, seeing they crucify to themselves the Son of God afresh, and put Him to an open shame' [*Heb* 6:6]; and against the blood of the covenant, and the Spirit graciously offering to apply these things – 'Of how much sorer punishment, suppose ye, shall he be thought worthy, who hath trodden under foot the Son of God, and hath counted the blood of the covenant, wherewith he was sanctified, an unholy thing, and hath done despite unto the Spirit of grace?' [*Heb* 10:29.]

2. In the description, consider the qualifications of this object. It is singularly made out to the party by the Spirit of God, both in the truth and good thereof. This saith (1) That there must be knowledge of the truth and way of salvation. The Pharisees knew that Christ was the heir – 'But when they saw the Son, they said among themselves, This is the heir, come, let us kill Him.' [*Matt* 21:38.] The party hath knowledge – 'But if we sin wilfully after that we have received the knowledge of the truth, there remaineth no more sacrifice for sins.' [*Heb* 10:26.] (2) That knowledge of the thing must not swim only in the head, but there must be some half-heart persuasion of it: Christ knew the Pharisees' thoughts [*Matt* 12:25]; and so did judge them, and that the contrary of what they spake was made out upon their heart. There is a *tasting*, which is beyond simple enlightening – 'For it is impossible for those who were once enlightened, and have tasted of the heavenly gift, and have tasted of the good word of God,

and of the powers of the world to come,' etc. [*Heb* 6:4, 5.] Yea, there is such a persuasion ordinarily as leadeth to a deal of outward sanctification – 'Who hath counted the blood of the covenant, wherewith he was sanctified, an unholy thing.' [*Heb* 10:29.] (3) This persuasion must not only be of the verity of the thing, but of the good of it: the party 'tasteth the good word of God, and the powers of the world to come' [*Heb* 6:5]; and he apprehendeth the thing as eligible. (4) This persuasion is not made out only by strength of argument, but also by an enlightening work of God's Spirit, shining on the truth, and making it conspicuous; therefore is that sin called, 'The sin against the Holy Ghost.' [*Matt* 12:31; *Mark* 3:29.] The persons are said 'to have been made partakers of the Holy Ghost' [*Heb* 6:4]; and 'to do despite unto the Spirit of grace,' who was in the nearest step of a gracious operation with them. [*Heb* 10:29.]

3. In this description, consider the acting of the party against the object so qualified. It is a rejecting and opposing of it; which importeth (1) That men have once, some way at least, been in hands with it, or had the offer of it, as is true of the Pharisees. (2) That they do reject, even with contempt, what they had of it, or in their offer. The Pharisees deny it, and speak disdainfully of Christ – 'This fellow doth not cast out devils, but by Beelzebub, the prince of the devils.' [*Matt* 12:24.] They fall away, intending to put Christ to 'an open shame.' [*Heb* 6:6.] (3) The men set themselves against it by the spirit of persecution, as the Pharisees did still. They rail against it; therefore it is called 'blasphemy against the Holy Ghost.' [*Matt* 12:24, 31.] They would 'crucify Christ again' if they could. [*Heb* 6:6.] They are *adversaries*. [Heb 10:27.]

4. Consider the properties of this acting. (1) It is *avowed*, that is, not seeking to shelter or to hide itself. The Pharisees speak against Christ publicly – 'But when the Pharisees heard it, they said, This fellow doth not cast out devils, but by Beelzebub the prince of the devils.' [*Matt* 12:24.] They would have 'Christ brought to an open shame.' [*Heb* 6:6.] They forsake the ordinances which savour that way – 'Not forsaking the assembling of ourselves together, as the manner of some is' – and despise the danger; for, looking for indignation, they trample that blood still. [*Heb* 10:25, 27, 29.] (2) The party acteth *freely*. It is not from unadvisedness, nor from force or constraint, but an acting of free choice; nothing doth force the Pharisees to speak against and persecute Christ. They 'crucify to themselves,' they re-act the murder of their own free accord, and in their own bosom, none constraining them. They sin of free choice, or, as the word may be rendered, *spontaneously* – 'For if we sin wilfully, after that we have received the knowledge of the truth, there remaineth no more sacrifice for sins.' [*Heb* 6:6; 10:26.] (3) It is acted *wilfully*. They are so resolute, they will not be dissuaded by any offer, or the most precious means, as is clear in the aforesaid scriptures. (4) It is done *maliciously*, so that it proceeds not so much, if at all, from a temptation to pleasure, profit, or honour. It proceedeth not from fear, or force, or from any good end proposed, but out of heart-malice against God and Christ, and the advancement of His glory and kingdom: so that it is of the very nature of Satan's sin, who hath an irreconcilable hatred against God, and the remedy of sin, because His glory is thereby advanced. This is a special ingredient in this sin. The Pharisees are found guilty of heart-malice against Christ, since they spake so

against Him, and not against their own children's casting out devils: and this is the force of Christ's argument – 'If I, by Beelzebub, cast out devils, by whom do your children cast them out?' [*Matt* 12:27.] They do their utmost 'to crucify Christ again, and to bring Him to an open shame.' [*Heb* 6:6.] They are *adversaries*, like the devil. (5) It is done *despitefully*: the malice must bewray itself. The Pharisees must proclaim that Christ hath correspondence with devils: He must 'be put to open shame, and crucified again': they must 'tread under foot that blood, and do despite to the Spirit': so that the party had rather perish a thousand times than be in Christ's debt for salvation.

5. The *last* thing in the description is, the ordinary attendant or consequence of this sin; it induceth *desperate and hopeless fear*. They fear Him, whom they hate with a slavish, hopeless fear, such as devils have – 'A certain fearful looking for of judgment, and fiery indignation, which shall devour the adversaries.' [*Heb* 10:27.] They know that God will put out His power against them; they tremble in the remembrance of it; and if they could be above Him, and destroy Him, they would: and since they cannot reach that, they hate with the utmost of heart-malice, and do persecute Him, and all that is His, with despite.

[3] *Conclusions bearing on the objection*

As for the *third* thing proposed, viz., the *conclusions* to be drawn from what is said, whereby we will speak directly to the objection. (1) As I hinted before, since the sin against the Holy Ghost is so remarkable, and may be well known where it is, none should charge themselves with it, unless they can prove and establish the charge; for it is a great wrong done unto God to labour to persuade my soul that He will never pardon me: it is the very way to make me desperate, and to lead me into the unpardonable sin; therefore, unless thou canst and dare say that thou dost hate the way which God has devised for the saving of sinners, and dost resolve to oppose the thriving of His kingdom, both with Himself and others, out of malice and despite against God, thou oughtest not to suspect thyself guilty of this sin. (2) Whatsoever thou hast done against God, if thou dost repent of it, and wish it were undone, thou canst not be guilty of this sin; for in it heart-malice and despite against God do still prevail. (3) If thou art content to be His debtor for pardon, and would be infinitely obliged unto Him for it, then thou canst not, in this case, be guilty of the sin against the Holy Ghost; for, as we showed before, they who are guilty of it do so despite God that they would not be His debtors for salvation. (4) Whatsoever thou hast done, if thou hast a desire after Jesus Christ, and dost look with a sore heart after Him, and cannot think of parting with His blessed company for ever, or, if thou must part with Him, yet dost wish well to Him, and all His, thou needest not suspect thyself to be guilty of this unpardonable sin; for there can be no such hatred of Him in thy bosom as is necessarily required to make up that sin. (5) If thou would be above the reach of that sin, and secure against it for ever, then go work up thy heart to approve of salvation by Christ Jesus, and so close with God in Him, acquiescing in Him as the sufficient ransom and rest, as we have been pressing before, and yield to Him to be saved in His way. Do this in good earnest, and thou shalt for ever be put out of the reach of that awful thing wherewith Satan doth affright so many poor seekers of God.

6 THE WANT OF POWER TO BELIEVE CONSIDERED AS A HINDRANCE

Objection: Although I be not excluded from the benefit of the new covenant, yet it is not in my power to believe on Christ; for faith is the gift of God, and above the strength of flesh and blood.

Answer: It is true that saving faith, by which alone a man can heartily close with God in Christ, is above our power and is the gift of God, as we said before in the premises; yet remember (1) The Lord hath left it as a duty upon all who hear this gospel cordially by faith to close with His offer of salvation through Christ, as is clear from Scripture. And you must know, that although it be not in our power to perform that duty of ourselves, yet the Lord may justly condemn us for not performing it, and we are inexcusable; because at first he made man perfectly able to do whatsoever He should command. (2) The Lord commanding this thing, which is above our power, willeth us to be sensible of our inability to do the thing, and would have us to put it on Him to work it in us. He hath promised to give the new heart, and He hath not excluded any from the benefit of that promise. (3) The Lord uses, by these commands and invitations, and men's meditation on the same, and their supplication about the thing, to convey power unto the soul to perform the duty.

Therefore, for answer to the objection, I do entreat thee, in the Lord's name, to lay to heart these His commandments and promises, and meditate on them, and upon that blessed business of the new covenant, and pray unto God, as you can, over them, 'for He will be inquired of to do these things' [*Ezek* 36:37]; and lay thy cold heart to that device of God expressed in the Scripture, and unto Christ Jesus, who is given for a covenant to the people, and look to Him for life and quickening. Go and endeavour to approve of that salvation in the way God doth offer it, and so close with, and rest on Christ for it, as if all were in thy power; yet, looking to Him for the thing, as knowing that it must come from Him; and if thou do so, He who meets those who remember Him in His ways [*Is* 64:5], will not be wanting on His part; and thou shalt not have ground to say, that thou movedst toward the thing until thou couldst do no more for want of strength, and so left it at God's door. It shall not fail on His part, if thou have a mind for the business; yea, I may say, if by all thou hast ever heard of that matter, thy heart loveth it, and desireth to be engaged with it, thou hast it already performed within thee; so that difficulty is past before thou wast aware of it.

7 UNFRUITFULNESS A HINDRANCE

Objection: Many who have closed with Christ Jesus, as aforesaid, are still complaining of their leanness and fruitlessness, which makes my heart lay the less weight on that duty of believing.

Answer: If thou be convinced that it is a duty to believe on Christ, you may not neglect it under any pretence. As for the complaints of some who have looked after Him, not admitting every one to be judge of his own fruit, I say –

1. Many, by their jealousies of God's love, and by their unbelief, after they have so closed with God, do obstruct many precious communications, which otherwise would be let out to them – 'And He did not

many mighty works there because of their unbelief.' [*Matt* 13:58.]

2. It cannot be that any whose heart is gone out after Christ 'have found Him a wilderness.' [*Jer* 2:31.] Surely they find somewhat in their spirit swaying them towards God in those two great things, namely, how to be found in Him in that day – 'Yea, doubtless, and I count all things but loss for the excellency of the knowledge of Christ Jesus my Lord; for whom I have suffered the loss of all things, and do count them but dung, that I may win Christ and be found in Him; not having mine own righteousness, which is of the law, but that which is through the faith of Christ, the righteousness which is of God by faith' [*Phil* 3:8, 9]; and how to show forth His praise in the land of the living, 'Deal bountifully with thy servant, that I may live and keep Thy word.' [*Ps* 119:17.] 'Wilt Thou not deliver my feet from falling, that I may walk before God in the land of the living.' [*Ps* 56:13.] They find these two things existing in the soul, and that is much. Moreover, they shall, on due inquiry, ever find such an emptiness in the creatures, that the utmost abundance of the creature cannot satisfy their souls – all is vanity, only God can fill the empty room in their heart; and when He breathes but a little, there is no room for additional comfort from creatures. This shows that God has captivated the man, and hath fixed that saving principle in the understanding and heart – 'Who is God but the Lord? Worship Him, all ye gods.' [*Ps* 97:7.] Yea, further, those whose hearts have closed with God in Christ as aforesaid, will not deny that there hath been seasonable preventings and quickenings now and then when the soul was like to fail – 'For Thou preventest me with the blessings of Thy goodness.' [*Ps* 21:3.] 'When

I said, My foot slippeth, Thy mercy, O Lord, held me up. In the multitude of my thoughts within me, Thy comforts delight my soul.' [*Ps* 94:18, 19.] Therefore, let none say that there is no fruit following, and let none neglect their duty upon the unjust and groundless complaints of others.

8 IGNORANCE CONCERNING PERSONAL COVENANTING A HINDRANCE – THE NATURE OF THAT DUTY

Objection: Although I judge it my duty to close with God's device in the covenant, I am in the dark how to manage that duty; for sometimes God offers to be our God without any mention of Christ, and sometimes saith, that He will betroth us unto Him: and in other places of Scripture we are called to come to Christ, and He is the bridegroom. Again, God sometimes speaketh of Himself as a Father to men, sometimes as a Husband; Christ is sometimes called the Husband, and sometimes a Brother; which relations seem inconsistent, and do much put me in the dark how to apprehend God, when my heart would agree with Him and close with Him.

Answer: It may be very well said, that men do come to God, or close with Him, and yet they come to Christ, and close with Him. They may be said to come under a marriage-relation unto God, and unto Christ also, who is husband, father, brother, etc., to them; and there is no such mystery here as some do conceive.

For the better understanding of it, consider these few things. 1. Although God made man perfect at the beginning, and put him in some capacity of transacting with Him immediately – 'God hath made man upright' [*Eccles*

7:29]; 'And the Lord God commanded the man, saying, Of every tree of the garden thou mayest freely eat,' etc. [*Gen* 2:16, 17]; yet man by his fall did put himself at such a distance from God, as to be in an utter incapacity to bargain or deal any more with Him immediately.

2. The Lord did, after Adam's fall, make manifest the new covenant, in which He did signify he was content to transact with man again, in and through a Mediator; and so did appoint men to come to Him through Christ – 'He is able to save them to the uttermost that come unto God by Him' [*Heb* 7:25]; and to look for acceptance only in Him – 'To the praise of the glory of His grace, wherein he hath made us accepted in the Beloved' [*Eph* 1:6]; ordaining men to hear Christ, He being the only party in whom God was well pleased – 'This is my beloved Son, in whom I am well pleased, hear ye Him.' [*Matt* 17:5.]

3. This matter is so clear, and supposed to be so evident in the Scripture, and so manifest to all who are under the ordinances, that the Lord often speaks of transacting with Himself, not making mention of the Mediator, because it is supposed that every one in the church knows that now there is no dealing with God, except by and through Christ Jesus the Mediator.

4. Consider that Christ Jesus, God-man, is not only a fit place of meeting for God and men to meet in, and a fit spokesman to treat between the parties now at variance – 'God was in Christ reconciling the world to Himself' [2 *Cor* 5:19]; but we may say also, He is an immediate bridegroom; and so our closing or transacting with God may be justly called *the marriage of the King's son*, and the elect may be called *the Lamb's wife*; Christ Jesus being, as it were, the hand which God holdeth out to men, and

on which they lay hold when they deal with God. And so through and by Christ we close with God, as our God, on whom our soul doth terminate lastly and ultimately through Christ 'Who by Him do believe in God that raised Him from the dead, and gave Him glory, that your faith and hope might be in God.' [1 *Peter* 1:21.]

5. Consider that the various relations mentioned in Scripture are set down to signify the sure and indissoluble union and communion between God and His people. Whatsoever connexion is between head and members, root and branches, king and subjects, shepherd and flock, father and children, brother and brother, husband and wife, etc., all is here – 'And they all shall be one, as Thou, Father, art in me, and I in Thee; that they also may be one in us; that the world may believe that Thou hast sent me. And the glory which Thou gavest me I have given them: that they may be one, even as we are one. I in them, and Thou in me, that they may be perfect in one, and that the world may know that Thou hast sent me, and hast loved them, as Thou hast loved me. And I have declared unto them Thy name, and will declare it: that the love wherewith Thou hast loved me may be in them, and I in them.' [*John* 17:21–26.] So that whatsoever is spoken in Scripture, people may be sure, that God calleth them to be reconciled unto Him through Christ, and doth offer Himself to be their God and husband in Him alone: and men are to accept God to be their God in Christ, approving of that way of relief for poor man, and to give up themselves unto God in Christ, in whom alone they can be accepted. And they who close with Christ, they do close with God and Him, who is in Christ, 'reconciling the world to Himself.' [2 *Cor* 5:19; *John* 14:8–11.] And we are not to dip further into the different relations mentioned

in Scripture between God or Christ and men, than as they may point out union and communion, or nearness with God through Christ Jesus, and our advantage thereby.

These things being clear, we will not multiply words: but since to believe on Christ is the great duty required of all that hear this gospel, we entreat every one, in the Lord's name, to whom the report of this shall come, that without delay they take to heart their lost condition in themselves, and that they lay to heart the remedy which God hath provided by Jesus Christ, whereof He hath made a free offer unto all who will be content with the same, and to be saved that way; and that they lay to heart, that there is no other way of escape from the wrath that is to come, because of which men would be glad, at the last day, to run into a lake of melted lead, to be hid from the face of the Lamb, whom they do here despise; we say, we entreat all, in the consideration of these things, to work up their hearts to this business, and to lay themselves open for God, and to receive Him through Christ in the offers of the gospel, acquiescing in Him as the only desirable and satisfying good, that so they may secure themselves. Go speedily and search for His offers of peace and salvation in the Scripture, and work up your heart and soul to close with them, and with Christ in them, and with God in Christ; and do it so, as you may have this to say, that you were serious, and in earnest, and cordial here, as ever you were in any thing to your apprehension; and, for aught you know, Christ is the choice of your heart, at least you neither know nor allow anything to the contrary; whereupon your heart doth appeal unto God, to search and try if there be aught amiss, to rectify it, and lead you into the right way.

Now, this cleaving of the heart unto Him, and casting itself upon Him to be saved in His way, is believing; which doth, indeed, secure a man from the wrath that is to come, because now he hath received Christ, and believeth on Him, and so shall not enter into condemnation, as saith the Scripture.

9 DOUBTS AS TO THE INQUIRER'S BEING SAVINGLY IN COVENANT WITH GOD ANSWERED

Objection: When I hear what it is to believe on Christ Jesus, I think sometimes I have faith; for I daresay, to my apprehension, I approve of the plan of saving sinners by Christ Jesus; my heart goeth out after Him, and doth terminate upon Him as a satisfying treasure; and I am glad to accept God to be my God in Him: but I often question if ever I have done so, and so am, for the most part, kept hesitating and doubting if I do believe, or am savingly in covenant with God.

Answer: It is not unusual for many, whose hearts are gone out after Christ in the gospel, and have received Him, to bring the same in question again: therefore I shall advise one thing, as a notable help to fix the soul in the maintaining of faith and an interest in God, and that is, that men not only close heartily with God in Christ, as aforesaid, but also that they expressly, explicitly, by word of mouth and *viva voce*, formally close with Christ Jesus, and accept God's offer of salvation through Him, and so make a covenant with God. And this, by God's blessing, may contribute not a little for establishing them concerning their saving interest in God.

CHAPTER IV

Concerning personal covenanting with God in Christ

1 CERTAIN THINGS PREMISED CONCERNING PERSONAL COVENANTING

Before I speak directly to this express covenanting with God, I premise these few things: 1. I do not here intend a covenanting with God essentially differing from the covenant between God and the visible church, as the Lord doth hold it out in His revealed will; neither do I intend a covenant differing essentially from the transacting of the heart with God in Christ, formerly spoken unto: it is that same covenant; only it differeth by a singular circumstance, namely, the *formal expression* of the thing which the heart did before practise.

2. I grant this express covenanting and transacting with God is not absolutely necessary for a man's salvation; for if any person close heartily and sincerely with God, offering Himself in Christ in the gospel, his soul and state are thereby secured, according to the Scripture, although he utter not words with his mouth; but this express verbal covenanting with God is very expedient, for the better wellbeing of a man's state, and for his more comfortable maintaining of an interest in Christ Jesus.

3. This express covenanting with God by word of mouth is of no worth without sincere heart-closing with God in Christ joined with it; for, without that, it is but a profaning of the Lord's name, and a mocking of Him to

His face, so 'to draw near unto Him with the lips, whilst the heart is far from Him.'

4. I grant both cordial and verbal transacting with God will not make out a man's gracious state unto him, so as to put and keep it above controversy, without the joint witness of the Spirit, by which we know what is freely given to us of God; yet this explicit way of transacting with God, joined with that heart-closing with Him in Christ, contributes much for clearing up to a man that there is a fixed bargain between God and him, and will do much to ward off from him many groundless jealousies and objections of an unstable mind and heart, which useth with shame to deny this hour what it did really act and perform the former hour. This explicit covenanting is as an instrument taken of what passed between God and the soul, and so hath its own advantage for strengthening of faith.

As for this express covenanting, we shall – (1) Show that it is a very warrantable practice. (2) We shall show shortly what is previously required of those who do so transact with God. (3) How men should go about that duty. (4) What should follow thereupon.

[1] *The thing itself is warrantable*

As to the *first*, I say, it is a warrantable practice and an incumbent duty, expressly and by word to covenant with God; which appeareth thus:

1. In many places of Scripture, if we look to what they may bear, according to their scope and the analogy of faith, God hath commanded it, and left it on people as a duty – 'One shall say, I am the Lord's.' 'Surely shall one say, In the Lord have I righteousness and strength.' [*Is* 44:5; 45:24.] 'Wilt thou not from this time cry unto Me,

My Father, Thou are the guide of my youth.' [*Jer* 3:4.] 'They shall say, the Lord is my God' [*Zech* 13:9]; 'Thou shalt call Me Ishi' [*Hos* 2:16]; and in many places elsewhere. Now, since God hath so clearly left it on men in the letter of the word, they may be persuaded that it is a practice warranted and allowed by Him, and well-pleasing unto Him.

2. It is the approved practice of the saints in Scripture thus expressly to covenant with God, and they have found much comfort in that duty afterwards. David did often expressly say unto God, that He was his God, his portion, and that himself was His servant. Thomas will put his interest out of question with it – 'And Thomas answered and said unto Him, My Lord and my God.' [*John* 20:28.] Yea, I say, the saints are much quieted in remembrance of what hath passed that way between God and them – 'Whom have I in heaven but Thee? and there is none upon earth that I desire besides Thee.' 'I cried unto Thee, O Lord; I said, Thou art my refuge, and my portion in the land of the living.' [*Ps* 73:25; 142:5.] We find it often so in the book of the Canticles. Now, shall the chief worthies of God abound so much in a duty, which produces so much peace and satisfaction to them in many cases, and shall we, under the New Testament, unto whom access is ministered abundantly, and who partake of the sap of the olive; shall we, I say, fall behind in this approved method of communion with God? Since we study to imitate that cloud of witnesses in other things, as faith, zeal, patience, etc., let us also imitate them in this.

3. The thing about which we here speak is a matter of the greatest concernment in all the world. 'It is the life of our soul.' [*Deut* 32:47.] Oh! shall men study to be

express, explicit, plain, and peremptory, in all their other great businesses, because they are such: and shall they not much more be peremptory and express in this, which doth most concern them? I wonder that many not only do not speak it with their mouth, but that they do not swear and subscribe it with their hand, and do not everything for securing of God to themselves in Christ, and themselves unto God, which the Scriptures doth warrant – 'One shall say, I am the Lord's; and another shall call himself by the name of Jacob; and another shall subscribe with his hand unto the Lord, and surname himself by the name of Israel.' [*Is* 44:5.]

This also may have its own weight, as an argument to press this way of covenanting with God, that the business of an interest in Christ, and of real and honest transacting with Him, is a thing which, in the experience of saints, is most frequently brought into debate and in question; therefore, men had need all the ways they can, even by thought, word, and deed, to put it to a point.

This also may be urged here for pressing this as a duty, that God is so formal, express, distinct, and legal, to say so, in all the business of man's salvation, namely, Christ must be a near kinsman to whom the right of redemption doth belong; He must be chosen, called authorized, and sent; covenants formally drawn between the Father and Him, the Father accepting payment and satisfaction, giving formal discharges, all done clearly and expressly. Shall the Lord be so express, plain, and peremptory in every part of the business, and shall our part of it rest in a confused thought, and we be as dumb beasts before Him? If it were a marriage between man and wife, it would not be judged enough, although there were consent in heart given by the woman, and known to the man, if she did never express so much by word, being in a capacity to do so. Now, this covenant between God and man is held out in Scripture as a marriage between man and wife – 'And I will betroth thee unto Me for ever; yea, I will betroth thee unto Me in righteousness, and in judgment, and in loving-kindness, and in mercies: I will even betroth thee unto Me in faithfulness; and thou shalt know the Lord.' [*Hos* 2:19, 20.] 'For I am jealous over you with godly jealousy; for I have espoused you to one husband, that I may present you as a chaste virgin to Christ.' [2 *Cor* 11:2.] The whole Song of Solomon speaketh it. The Lord useth similitudes, to signify unto us what He intends; and surely this is a special requisite in marriage, that the wife give an express and explicit consent unto the business: the man saith – 'So I take thee to be my lawful wife, and do oblige myself to be a dutiful husband.' The woman is obliged, on the other part, to express her consent, and to say – 'Even so I take thee to be my lawful husband, and do promise duty and subjection.' It is so here; the Lord saith, 'I do betroth thee unto me in faithfulness, and thou shalt call me Ishi,' that is, my husband. [*Hos* 2:16.] I will be for thee as a head and husband, if 'thou wilt not be for another.' [*Hos* 3:3.] The man ought to answer, and say, Amen, so be it; Thou shalt be my God, my Head, and Lord, and I shall and will be Thine, and not for another — 'I am my beloved's, and my beloved is mine.' [*Cant* 6:3.] And so this making of the covenant with God is called 'a giving of the hand to Him,' as the word is – 'Now be ye not stiff-necked, as your fathers were, but yield yourselves unto the Lord, and enter into His sanctuary, which He hath sanctified for ever; and serve the Lord your God, that the fierceness of His wrath may turn away from you' [2 *Chron* 30:8]; which doth intimate a very express, formal, explicit, and positive bargaining with God. So then, we conclude it to be an incumbent duty, and an approved practice necessary for the quieting of a man's mind, and his more comfortable being in covenant with God, and more fully answering God's condescension and offer in that great and primary promise – 'I will be your God, and ye shall be my people.'

Not only may and should people thus expressly close with God in Christ for fixing their heart; but they may upon some occasions renew this verbal transaction with God, especially when, through temptations, they are made to question if they have really and sincerely closed covenant with God. As they are then to put out new acts of faith, embracing Christ as the desirable portion and treasure, and also upon other occasions, so it were expedient, especially if there remain any doubt as to the thing, that by *viva voce* and express words they determine that controversy, and 'say of the Lord, and to Him, that He is their refuge and portion' [*Ps* 91:2; 142:5.] We find the saints doing so, and we may imitate them. Especially,

1. In the time of great backsliding, people were wont to renew the covenant with God, and we should do so also. Our heart should go out after Christ in the promises of reconciliation with God: for He is our peace upon all occasions, and our Advocate; and we are bound to apprehend Him so, when we transgress – 'If any man sin, we have an Advocate with the Father, Jesus Christ the righteous' [1 *John* 2:1]; and to express so much by word, as the saints did in their formal renewing of the covenant.

2. When people are in hazard, and difficulties are present or foreseen, then it were good that they should send out their hearts after Him, and express their adherence unto Him for securing their own hearts. We find Joshua

doing so, when he was to settle in the land of Canaan, in the midst of snares: 'Now therefore, fear the Lord, and serve Him in sincerity and in truth, and put away the gods which your fathers served on the other side of the flood, and in Egypt; and serve ye the Lord. And if it seem evil unto you to serve the Lord, choose you this day whom ye will serve; whether the gods which your fathers served, that were on the other side of the flood, or the gods of the Amorites, in whose land ye dwell: but as for me and my house, we will serve the Lord. And the people answered and said, God forbid that we should forsake the Lord to serve other gods; for the Lord our God, He it is that brought us up and our fathers out of the land of Egypt, from the house of bondage, and which did those great signs in our sight, and preserved us in all the way wherein we went, and among all the people through whom we passed; and the Lord drave out from before us all the people, even the Amorites which dwelt in the land: therefore will we also serve the Lord; for He is our God. And Joshua said unto the people, Ye cannot serve the Lord: for He is an holy God; He will not forgive your transgressions nor your sins. If ye forsake the Lord, and serve strange gods, then He will turn and do you hurt, and consume you, after that He hath done you good. And the people said unto Joshua, Nay; but we will serve the Lord. And Joshua said unto the people, Ye are witnesses against yourselves, that ye have chosen you the Lord, to serve Him. And they said, We are witnesses. Now, therefore put away (said he) the strange gods which are among you, and incline your heart unto the Lord God of Israel. And the people said unto Joshua, the Lord our God will we serve, and His voice will we obey. So Joshua made a covenant with the people that day, and set them a statute and an ordinance in Shechem.' [*Josh* 24.] So did David in his straits – 'In the shadow of thy wings will I make my refuge, until these calamities be overpast.' [*Ps* 57:1.]

3. When men apprehend God to be at a distance from them, and their soul to be under withering and decay, then it is safest heartily to close with Christ, and embrace Him by faith for the securing of the soul; and it were good to put it out of question by the expression of the thing. This is the ready way to draw sap from Christ the root, for recovering of the soul, and for establishing the heart before Him. The spouse, in the Song of Solomon, doth so; thus asserting her interest in Him when in such a condition, professing and avowing Him to be her beloved. [*Cant* 5.]

4. At the celebration of the Lord's Supper, men should thus cordially close with God in Christ, and speak and express so much; for that is a feast of love; and then and there we come under a solemn professing of closing with God in Christ personally and openly, and to receive the seal of it. It is, therefore, especially proper, at that time, to bring up both heart and tongue to second and answer our profession, and resigning over ourselves to be His, and at His disposing.

We shall not confine the Lord's people to times and seasons for this duty; the Lord may bind it upon them at His pleasure; only there is hazard, that by too frequent express covenanting with God, men turn too formal in it. Therefore, it is not so fit that people should ordinarily at full length renew that explicit transaction with God, but rather to declare unto God that they adhere unto the covenant made with Him, and that they do maintain and will never revoke nor recall the same; and withal, they may hint the sum of it, in laying claim unto God in Christ as their own God; and this they may do often, even in all their addresses to God. And probably this is the thing designed by the saints in their so ordinary practice in Scripture, whilst they assert their interest in God as their God and portion; and it is fit that men, in all their walk, hold their heart to the business, by heart-cleaving to God in Christ – 'The life we live in the flesh should be by faith in the Son of God.' [*Gal* 2:20.]

[2] *The preparation needed*

As to the *second* thing, namely, what preparation is required of him who is expressly to transact with God here. Besides what we mentioned before, as previous to a man's closing with Christ Jesus, we only add (1) That he who would explicitly bargain with God, must know, that to do so is warranted, and allowed by God, as we showed before. If this be wanting, a man cannot do it in faith, and so it will be sin unto him – 'Whatsoever is not of faith is sin.' [*Rom* 14:23.] (2) The man must labour to bring up his heart to the thing, that it do not belie the tongue; it will be a great mocking of God, so to 'draw near to Him with the lips, whilst the heart is far from Him.' [*Is* 29:13.]

[3] *How the duty of covenanting is to be performed*

The *third* thing to be considered in this express verbal covenanting with God is, the way how it is to be performed and managed. And besides what was said before in heart-closing with Christ, I add here:

1. The man should do it *confidently*; not only believing that he is about his duty when he doth it; but also, that God in Christ Jesus will accept his poor imperfect way of doing his duty: He doth 'accept a man according to

what he hath, if there be a willing mind.' [2 *Cor* 8:12.] A mite is accepted, since it is 'all the poor woman's substance.' [*Mark* 12:44.] Yea, if it can be attained, the man should believe that the issue and consequence of this transacting shall prove comfortable, and all shall be well; and that God, who engageth for all in the covenant (since He has determined the man to this happy choice), will in some measure make him forthcoming, and will perfect what concerns him – 'Faithful is He that calleth you, who also will do it.' [1 *Thess* 5:24.] If this confidence be wanting, the matter will be done with much fear and jealousy, if not worse: and will still prove a disquieting business to the man.

2. It should be done holily. It is called 'the holy covenant' [*Luke* 1:72]; 'the sure mercies (or holy things) of David.' [*Acts* 13:34.] Here it were fitting that what is done in this express transacting with God should not be done cursorily and by the bye, but in some special address unto God; the thing should be spoken unto the Lord – 'I cried unto Thee, O Lord; I said, Thou art my refuge and my portion.' [*Ps* 142:5.] It is proper, in so great a business, that a portion of time were set apart for confession and supplication before God; yea, also, the person so transacting with God should labour to have high apprehensions of God's greatness and sovereignty – 'Thou art great, O Lord God; for there is none like unto Thee, neither is there any God beside Thee,' [2 *Sam* 7:22.] although He thus humble himself to behold things in heaven and earth. And these high and holy thoughts of Him will and should be attended with abasing and humbling thoughts of self, although admitted to this high dignity – 'Then went King David in, and sat before the Lord: and he said, Who am I, O Lord God; and what is

my house that Thou hast brought me hitherto?' [2 *Sam* 7:18.] It is no small thing to be allied unto, and with, the great God of heaven and His Son Christ; as David speaketh, when King Saul did offer his daughter to him. [1 *Sam* 18:23.] Yea, further, there should be special guarding and watching that the heart keep spiritual in transacting with God. There is great reason for this holy way of performing the duty; for men are ready to mistake themselves, and to think of the Lord according to their own fancy, and to turn carnal in the business, since it is a marriage transaction held out in all the ordinary expressions of love, as in the Song of Solomon. [*Is* 62:5; *Zeph* 3:17.]

[4] *What should follow this solemn act*

The *fourth* thing we shall speak a word unto is, What should follow upon this express verbal covenanting with God. I say, besides that union and communion with God in Christ, following upon believing, if a man explicitly by word transact with God –

1. He should thenceforth be singularly careful to abide close with God, in all manner of conversation; for, if a man thenceforth do anything unsuitable, he doth falsify his word before God, which will stick much in his conscience, and prove a *snare*. If a man henceforth forsake God, and take on him to dispose of himself, since he is not his own, and hath opened his mouth unto the Lord, he makes inquiry after vows, and devoureth that which is holy. [*Prov* 20:25.]

2. He who so transacteth with God should hold steadfast that determination and conclusion. It is a shame for a man whose heart hath closed with God, and whose mouth hath ratified and confirmed it solemnly before Him,

to contradict himself again, and to admit anything to the contrary; he ought boldly to maintain the thing against every enemy.

Then, let me entreat you, who desire to be established in the matter of your interest in God, that, with all convenience, you set apart a portion of time for prayer before God, and labouring to work up your heart to seriousness, affection, and the faith of the duty to make a covenant, and to transact with God by express word, after this manner:

'O Lord, I am a lost and fallen creature by nature, and by innumerable actual transgressions, which I do confess particularly before Thee this day: and although, being born within the visible church, I was from the womb in covenant with Thee, and had the same sealed to me in baptism; yet, for a long time, I have lived without God in the world, senseless and ignorant of my obligation by virtue of that covenant. Thou hast at length discovered to me, and impressed upon my heart, my miserable state in myself, and hast made manifest unto my heart the satisfying remedy Thou hast provided by Christ Jesus, offering the same freely unto me, upon condition that I would accept of the same, and would close with Thee as my God in Christ, warranting and commanding me, upon my utmost peril, to accept of this offer, and to flee unto Christ Jesus; yea, to my apprehension, now Thou hast sovereignly determined my heart, and formed it for Christ Jesus, leading it out after Him in the offers of the gospel, causing me to approach unto the living God, to close so with Him and to acquiesce in His offer, without any known guile. And that I may come up to that establishment of spirit in this matter, which should be to my comfort, and the praise of Thy glorious grace; therefore, I am here this day to put that matter out of question by express words before Thee, according to Thy will. And now I, unworthy as I am, do declare, that I believe that Christ Jesus, who was slain at Jerusalem, was the Son of God, and the Saviour of the world. I do believe that record, that there is life eternal for men in Him, and in Him only. I do this day in my heart approve and acquiesce in that device of saving sinners by Him, and do intrust my soul unto Him. I do accept of reconciliation with God through Him, and do close with Thee as my God in Him. I choose Him in all that He is, and all that may follow Him, and do resign up myself, and what I am, or have, unto Thee; desiring to be divorced from everything hateful unto Thee, and that without exception, or reservation, or anything inconsistent within my knowledge, or any intended reversion. Here I give the hand to Thee, and do take all things about me witnesses, that I, whatever I be, or have hitherto been, do accept of God's offer of peace through Christ; and do make a sure covenant with Thee this day, never to be reversed, hoping that Thou wilt make all things forthcoming, both on Thy part and mine, seriously begging, as I desire to be saved, that my corruptions may be subdued, and my neck brought under Thy sweet yoke in all things, and my heart made cheerfully to acquiesce in whatsoever Thou dost unto me, or with me, in order to these ends. Now, glory be unto Thee, O Father, who devised such a salvation, and gave the Son to accomplish it: Glory be to Christ Jesus, who, at so dear a rate, did purchase the outletting of that love from the Father's bosom, and through whom alone this access is granted, and in whom I am reconciled unto God, and honourably united unto Him, and am no more an enemy or stranger: Glory to the Holy Ghost, who did alarm me when I was destroying myself, and who did not only convince me of my danger, but did also open my eyes to behold the remedy provided in Christ; yea, and did persuade and determine my wicked heart to fall in love with Christ, as the enriching treasure; and this day doth teach me how to covenant with God, and how to appropriate to myself all the sure mercies of David, and blessings of Abraham, and to secure to myself the favour and friendship of God for ever. Now, with my soul, heart, head, and whole man, as I can, I do acquiesce in my choice this day, henceforth resolving not to be my own, but Thine; and that the care of whatsoever concerns me shall be on Thee, as my Head and Lord, protesting humbly, that failings on my part (against which I resolve, Thou knowest) shall not make void this covenant; for so hast Thou said, which I intend not to abuse, but so much the more to cleave close unto Thee, and I must have liberty to renew, ratify, and draw extracts of this transaction, as often as shall be needful. Now, I know Thy consent to this bargain stands recorded in Scripture, so that I need no new signification of it; and I, having accepted of Thy offer upon Thine own terms, will henceforth wait for what is good, and for Thy salvation in the end. As Thou art faithful, pardon what is amiss in my way of doing the thing, and accept me in my Lord Jesus Christ, in whom only I desire pardon. And in testimony hereof, I set to my seal that God is true, in declaring Him a competent Saviour.'

Let people covenant with God in fewer or more words, as the Lord shall dispose them – for we intend no exact form of words for any person – only it were fitting that men should before the Lord acknowledge their lost state in themselves, and the relief that is by Christ; and that they do declare that they accept of the same as it is offered in the gospel, and do thankfully rest satisfied with it, intrusting themselves henceforth wholly unto God, to be saved in His way, for which they wait according to His faithfulness.

If men would heartily and sincerely do this, it might, through the Lord's blessing, help to establish them against many fears and jealousies; and they might date some good thing from this day and hour, which might prove comfortable unto them when they fall in the dark afterwards, and even when many failings do stare them in the face, perhaps at the hour of death – 'These be the last words of David: Although my house be not so with God, yet He hath made with me an everlasting covenant, ordered in all things and sure; for this is all my salvation, and all my desire.' [2 *Sam* 23:5.] It is much if a man can appeal unto God, and say, Thou knowest there was a day and an hour when in such a place I did accept of peace through Christ, and did deliver up my heart to Thee, to write on it Thy whole law without exception; heaven and earth are witnesses of it – 'Remember the word unto Thy servant, upon which Thou hast caused me to hope.' [*Ps* 119:49.]

2 A WANT OF PROPER FEELING CONSIDERED AS AN OBSTACLE

Objection: I dare not venture to speak such words unto God, because I find not my heart coming up full length in affection and seriousness; so I should but lie unto God in transacting so with Him.

Answer: It is to be regretted that men's hearts do not, with intensity of desire and affection, embrace and welcome that blessed offer and portion. Yet, for answer to this objection, remember: 1. That in those to whom the Lord gives the new heart, forming Christ in them, the whole heart is not renewed; there is 'flesh and spirit lusting against each other, the one contrary unto the other, so that a man can neither do the good or evil he would do,' with full strength. [*Gal* 5:17.] It is well if there be a good part of the heart going out after Christ, desiring to close with Him on His own terms.

2. That there is often a rational love in the heart unto Christ Jesus, expressing itself by a respect to His commandments – 'This is the love of God, that we keep His commandments; and His commandments are not grievous' [1 *John* 5:3]; when there is not a sensible prevailing love which maketh the soul sick – 'I am sick of love.' [*Cant* 2:5.] Men must not always expect to find this. I say, then, although somewhat in your heart drawn back, yet if you can say that you are convinced of your lost state without Him, that you want a righteousness to cover your guilt, and that you want strength to stand out against sin, or to do what is pleasing before God, and that you also see fulness in Him; in both these respects, if you dare say that somewhat within your heart would fain embrace Him upon His own terms, and would have both righteousness for justification, and strength in order to sanctification; and that what is within you contradicting this, is in some measure your burden and your bondage – if it be so, your heart is brought up a tolerable length; go on to the business, and determine the matter by covenanting with God, and say with your mouth, 'That you have both righteousness and strength in the Lord,' as He hath sworn you shall do – 'I have sworn by Myself, the word is gone out of My mouth in righteousness, and shall not return, that unto Me every knee shall bow, every tongue shall

swear. Surely, shall one say, In the Lord have I righteousness and strength: even to Him shall men come; and all that are incensed against Him shall be ashamed.' [*Is* 45:23, 24.] It is according to Scripture to say unto God, I believe, when much unbelief is in me and the heart is divided in the case – 'Lord, I believe, help Thou mine unbelief.' [*Mark* 9:24.] Withal show unto God how matters are in your heart, so that you may be without guile before Him, concealing nothing from Him; and put your heart as it is in His hand, to write His law on it, according to the covenant: for that is the thing He seeks of men, that they deliver up their heart to Him, that He may stamp it with His whole will, without exception; and if you can heartily consent unto that, judging Christ's blood a sufficient ransom and satisfaction for man's transgression, you may go and expressly strike a covenant with God, for your heart and affection is already engaged.

3 THE FEAR OF BACKSLIDING A HINDRANCE TO COVENANTING

Objection: I dare not so covenant with God lest I break with Him; yea, I persuade myself, that if such a temptation did offer, so and so circumstantiated, I should fall before it: therefore, to transact so with God whilst I foresee such a thing, were but to aggravate my condemnation.

Answer: 1. You have already entered into covenant with God, as you are a member of His visible Church; and what is now pressed upon you is, that you more heartily, sincerely, particularly, and expressly covenant and transact with Him: you are already obliged heartily to close with God in Christ: and if you do it in heart, I hope the hazard is no greater by saying that you do so, or have done so.

2. What will you do if you decline sincerely closing with God in Christ, and do not accept of His peace as it is offered? You have no other way of salvation; either you must do this or perish for ever: and if you do it with your heart, you may also say it with your tongue.

3. If people may be afraid of covenanting with God lest they should afterwards transgress, then not one man should covenant with God; for surely every one will transgress afterwards, if they live any length of time after the transaction; and we know no way like this to secure men from falling; for if you covenant honestly with Him, He engageth, beside the new heart, to put His fear and law therein, to give His Spirit to cause you to walk in His way. And when you covenant with God, you deliver up yourself unto Him to be sanctified and made conformable to His will. It is rather a giving up of yourself to be led in His way, in all things, and kept from every evil way, than any formal engagement on your part to keep His way, and to hold off from evil: so that you need not be afraid of the covenant, the language whereof is, 'Wilt thou not be made clean?' [*Jer* 13:27.] And all that shun to join in covenant with God, do thereby declare that they desire not to be made clean.

4. As it is hard for any to say confidently they shall transgress, if such a temptation did offer, so and so circumstantiated, because that men may think that either God will keep a temptation out of their way, or will not suffer them to be tempted above what they are able to bear, or give to them a way of escape – 'God is our refuge and strength, a very present help in trouble.' [*Ps* 46:1.] 'There hath no temptation taken you, but such as is common to man: but God is faithful, who will not suffer

you to be tempted above what you are able to bear; but will with the temptation also make a way to escape, that ye may be able to bear it' [1 *Cor* 10:13]; so the question is not, what I may do afterwards, but what I now resolve to do. If my heart charge me at the present with any deceit or resolution to transgress, I must lay aside that deceit before I covenant with God; but if my heart charge me with no such purpose, yea, I dare say I resolve against every transgression; and although I think I shall fall before such and such temptation, yet that thought floweth not from any allowed and approved resolution to do so, but from a knowledge of my own corruption, and of what I have done to provoke God to desert me: but the Lord knows I resolve not to transgress, nor do I approve any secret inclination of my heart to such a sin, but would reckon it my singular mercy to be kept from sin in such a case; and I judge myself a wretched man, because of such a body of death within me, which threatens to make me transgress; in that case I say, My heart doth not condemn me, therefore, I may and ought to have confidence before God. [1 *John* 3:21.] If this then be the case, I say to thee, although thou shouldst afterwards fail many ways, and so perhaps hereby draw upon thyself sad temporal strokes, and lose for a season many expressions of His love, yet there is an 'Advocate with the Father' to plead thy pardon [1 *John* 2:1]; who hath satisfied for our breaches – 'He was wounded for our transgressions, He was bruised for our iniquities; the chastisement of our peace was upon Him, and with His stripes we are healed. All we like sheep have gone astray, we have turned every one to his own way, and the Lord hath laid on Him the iniquity of us all.' [*Is* 53:5, 6.] And for His sake God resolves to hold fast the covenant with men after their transgression – 'If his children forsake My law, and walk not in My judgments; if they break My statutes, and keep not My commandments: nevertheless My loving-kindness will I not utterly take from him, nor suffer My faithfulness to fail: my covenant will I not break, nor alter the thing that is gone out of My lips. Once have I sworn by My holiness.' [*Ps* 89 30–37.] Else how could He be said 'to betroth us to Himself for ever?' [*Hos* 2:19, 20.] And how could the covenant be called 'everlasting, ordered in all things and sure,' if there were not ground of comfort in it, 'even when our house is not so with God?' [2 *Sam* 23:5.]

Yea, it were not better than the covenant of works, if those who enter into it with God could so depart from Him again, as to make it void unto themselves, and to put themselves into a worse condition than they were in before they made it – 'And I will make an everlasting covenant with them, that I will not turn away from them, to do them good' [*Jer* 32:40] – compared with *Heb* 8:6, 'But now hath He obtained a more excellent ministry, by how much also He is the Mediator of a better covenant, which was established upon better promises.' 'The Lord hateth putting away.' [*Mal* 2:16.] No honest heart will stumble at this, but will rather be strengthened thereby in duty – 'I will heal their backsliding, I will love them freely; for mine anger is turned away from him. Who is wise, and he shall understand these things: prudent, and he shall know them? For the ways of the Lord are right, and the just shall walk in them.' [*Hos* 14:9.] For other ties and bonds, besides the fear of divorce, and punishment by death, do oblige the ingenuous wife unto duty; so here men will 'fear the Lord and His goodness.' [*Hos* 3:5.]

4 PAST EXPERIENCE OF FRUITLESSNESS CONSIDERED

Objection: I have at the celebration of the Lord's Supper, and on some other occasions, covenanted expressly and verbally with God; but my fruitlessness in His ways, and the renewed jealousies of my gracious state, make me question if ever I transacted with God in sincerity, and I think I can do it no otherwise than I have done it.

Answer: 1. Men are not to expect fruitfulness according to their desire, nor full assurance of God's favour immediately after they have fled unto Christ, and expressly transacted with God in Him; these things will keep a man at work all his days. The saints had their failings and shortcomings, yea, and backslidings, with many fits of dangerous unbelief, after they had very seriously and sincerely, and expressly closed with God, as their God in Christ.

2. Many do look for fruitfulness in their walk, and establishment of faith, from their own sincerity in transacting with God, rather than from the Spirit of the Lord Jesus. They fix their hearts on their own honesty and resolutions, and not in the blessed root, Christ Jesus, without whom we can do nothing, and are vanity altogether in our best estate. Men should remember, that one piece of grace cannot produce any degree of grace: Further, nothing can work grace but the arm of JEHOVAH: and if men would lean upon Christ, and covenant with Him as their duty absolutely, whatsoever may be the consequence, at least looking only to Him for the suitable fruit, it would fare better with them. God pleaseth not that men should betake themselves unto Christ, and

covenant with Him for a season until they see if such fruit and establishment shall follow, purposing to disclaim their interest in him and the covenant, if such and such fruit doth not appear within such a length of time. This is to put the ways of God to trial, and is very displeasing unto Him. Men must absolutely close with Christ, and covenant with Him, resolving to maintain these things as their duty, and a ready way to reach fruit, whatever shall follow thereupon; they having a testimony within them, that they seriously design conformity to His revealed will in all things; and that they have closed covenant with Him for the same end, as well as to be saved thereby.

3. Men should be sparing to bring in question their sincerity in transacting with God unless they can prove the same, or have great presumptions for it. If you can discover any deceit or guile in your transacting with Him, you are obliged to disclaim and rectify it, and to transact with God honestly, and without guile: but if you know nothing of your deceit or guile in the day you did transact with Him; yea, if you can say that you did appeal unto God in that day and that you dealt honestly with Him, and intended not to deceive; and did entreat Him, according to his faithfulness, to search and try if there was any crookedness in your way, and to discover it unto you, and heal it – 'Search me, O God, and know my heart: try me, and know my thoughts; and see if there be any wicked way in me, and lead me in the way everlasting' [*Ps* 139:23, 24]; and that afterwards you 'came to the light, that your deeds might be manifest' [*John* 3:20, 21]; and if you can say, that God's answers from His words to you, in so far as you could understand, were answers of peace, and confirmations of your sincerity; yea, further, if you dare say, that if, upon life and death, you were

again to transact with Him, you can do it no other way, nor intend more sincerity and seriousness than before; then I dare say unto thee in the Lord's name, thou ought not to question thy sincerity in transacting with God, but to 'have confidence before God, since thy heart doth not condemn thee' [1 *John* 3:21]; and thou art bound to believe that 'God dealeth uprightly with the upright man, and with the pure doth show Himself pure.' [*Ps* 18:25, 26.] If a man intend honestly, God will not suffer him to beguile Himself; yea, the Lord suffereth no man to deceive himself, unless the man intend to deceive both God and man.

4. Therefore impute your unfruitfulness to your unwatchfulness and your unbelief, and impute your want of full assurance unto an evil heart of unbelief, helped by Satan to act against the glorious free grace of God: and charge not these things to the want of sincerity in your closing with Christ. And resolve henceforth to abide close by the root, and you shall bring forth much fruit; and by much fruit you lay yourselves open to the witness of God's Spirit, which will testify with your spirit that you have sincerely and honestly closed with God, and that the rest of your works are wrought in God, and approved of Him; and so the witness of the Spirit and the water, joining with the blood, whereupon you are to lay the weight of your soul and conscience, and where alone you are to sink the curses of the law due unto you for all your sins and failings in your best things – these three do agree in one, namely, that this is the way of life and peace, and that you have interest therein, and so you come to quietness and full assurance – 'Abide in me, and I in you; as the branch cannot bear fruit of itself, except it abide in the vine, no more can ye, except ye abide in me. I am

the vine, ye are the branches; he that abideth in me, and I in him, the same bringeth forth much fruit; for without me ye can do nothing.' [*John* 15:4, 5.] 'He that hath my commandments and keepeth them, he it is that loveth me; and he that loveth me, shall be loved of my Father, and I will love him, and will manifest myself to him. If a man love me, he will keep my words; and my Father will love him, and we will come unto him, and make our abode with him.' [*John* 14:21, 23.] 'The Spirit itself beareth witness with our spirit that we are the children of God.' [*Rom* 8:16.] 'There are three that bear witness in earth, the spirit, and the water, and the blood; and these three agree in one.' [1 *John* 5:8.]

O blessed bargain of the new covenant, and thrice blessed Mediator of the same! Let Him ride prosperously and subdue nations and languages, and gather in all His jewels, that honourable company of the first-born, that stately troop of kings and priests, whose glory it shall be to have washed their garments in the blood of that spotless Lamb, and whose happiness shall continually flourish in following Him whithersoever He goeth, and in being in the immediate company of the Ancient of days, one sight of whose face shall make them in a manner forget that ever they were on the earth. Oh, if I could persuade men to believe that these things are not *yea* and *nay*, and to make haste towards Him, who hasteth to judge the world, and to call men to an account, especially concerning their improvement of this gospel! 'Even so, come Lord Jesus.'

CONCLUSION

The whole treatise resumed in a few questions and answers

Question 1: What is the great business a man hath to do in this world?

Answer: To make sure a saving interest in Christ Jesus, and to walk suitably thereto.

Question 2: Have not all the members of the visible church a saving interest in Christ?

Answer: No, verily; yea, but a very few of them have it.

Question 3: How shall I know if I have a saving interest in Him?

Answer: Ordinarily the Lord prepareth His own way in the soul by a work of humiliation, and discovereth a man's sin and misery to him, and exerciseth him so therewith, that he longs for the physician Christ Jesus.

Question 4: How shall I know if I have got a competent discovery of my sin and misery?

Answer: A competent sight of it makes a man take salvation to heart above anything in this world: it maketh him disclaim all relief in himself, even in his best things: it maketh Christ who is the Redeemer, very precious to the soul: it makes a man stand in awe to sin afterwards, and makes him content to be saved upon any terms God pleases.

Question 5: By what other ways may I discern a saving interest in Him?

Answer: By the going out of the heart seriously and

affectionately towards Him, as He is held out in the gospel; and this is faith or believing.

Question 6: How shall I know if my heart goes out after Him aright, and that my faith is true saving faith?

Answer: Where the heart goes out aright after Him in true and saving faith, the soul is pleased with Christ alone above all things, and is pleased with Him in all His three offices, to rule and instruct as well as to save; and is content to cleave unto Him, whatsoever inconveniences may follow.

Question 7: What other mark of a saving interest in Christ can you give me?

Answer: He that is in Christ savingly, is a new creature; He is graciously changed and renewed in some measure, in the whole man, and in all his ways pointing towards all the known commands of God.

Question 8: What if I find sin now and then prevailing over me?

Answer: Although every sin deserves everlasting vengeance, yet, if you be afflicted for your failings, confess them with shame of face unto God, resolving to strive against them honestly henceforth, and flee unto Christ for pardon, you shall obtain mercy, and your interest stands sure.

Question 9: What shall the man do who cannot lay claim to Christ Jesus nor any of those marks spoken of?

Answer: Let him not take rest until he make sure unto himself a saving interest in Christ.

Question 10: What way can a man make sure an interest in Christ, who never had a saving interest in Him hitherto?

Answer: He must take his sins to heart, and his great

hazard thereby, and he must take to heart God's offer of pardon and peace through Christ Jesus, and heartily close with God's offer by betaking himself unto Christ, the blessed refuge.

Question 11: What if my sins be singularly heinous, and great beyond ordinary?

Answer: Whatsoever thy sins be, if thou wilt close with Christ Jesus by faith, thou shalt never enter into condemnation.

Question 12: Is faith in Christ only required of men?

Answer: Faith is the only condition upon which God doth offer peace and pardon unto men; but be assured, faith, if it be true and saving, will not be alone in the soul, but will be attended with true repentance, and a thankful study of conformity to God's image.

Question 13: How shall I be sure that my heart doth accept God's offer, and doth close with Christ Jesus?

Answer: Go make a covenant expressly, and by word speak the thing unto God.

Question 14: What way shall I do that?

Answer: Set apart some portion of time, and, having considered your own lost estate, and the remedy offered by Christ Jesus, work up your heart to be pleased with and close with that offer, and say unto God expressly that you do accept of that offer, and of Him to be your God in Christ; and do give up yourself to Him to be saved in His way, without reservation or exception in any case; and that you henceforth will wait for salvation in the way He hath appointed.

Question 15: What if I break with God afterwards?

Answer: You must resolve in His strength not to break, and watch over your own ways, and put your heart in

His hand to keep it: and if you break, you must confess it unto God, and judge yourself for it, and flee to the Advocate for pardon, and resolve to do so no more: and this you must do as often as you fail.

Question: 16 How shall I come to full assurance of my interest in Christ, so that it may be beyond controversy?

Answer: Learn to lay your weight upon the blood of Christ, and study purity and holiness in all manner of conversation: and pray for the witness of God's Spirit to join with the blood and the water; and His testimony added unto these will establish you in the faith of an interest in Christ.

Question 17: What is the consequence of such closing with God in Christ by heart and mouth?

Answer: Union and communion with God, all good here, and His blessed fellowship in heaven for ever afterwards.

Question 18: What if I slight all these things, and do not lay them to heart to put them in practice?

Answer: The Lord cometh with His angels, in flaming fire, to render vengeance to them who obey not His gospel; and thy judgment shall be greater than that of Sodom and Gomorrah; and so much the greater that thou hast read this Treatise, for it shall be a witness against thee in that day.

APPENDIX

The extracts from the sermons of William Guthrie in the following pages are taken from the Appendix to the Melrose edition (1901) *of* The Christian's Great Interest, *which was edited by Alexander Smellie. Dr Smellie gleaned the extracts from a manuscript volume of Guthrie's sermons in the possession of the librarian of New College, Edinburgh.*

The contents of the volume consist mainly of sacramental discourses, preached in many different parts of the West of Scotland. Seventeen of Guthrie's discourses were published in Lectures and Sermons Preached in the Time of the Persecution, *a volume compiled by John Howie of Lochgoin.*

EXTRACTS FROM THE SERMONS OF WILLIAM GUTHRIE

'LEST THE GOD OF THIS WORLD BLIND US'

Look if the world, or anything in it, lays claim to the first-fruits of your labours daily. If it be first in your heart, or first in your hand, in the morning, it is your God; for a man's God claims his first thoughts, and ordinarily his last thoughts at night, and often his thoughts when he is sleeping. O, how few can say their 'sleep is sweet' unto them on a better account, and, 'when they awake, they are still with Him'!

Look if the world lays claim to your most precious time, which is devoted to a deity. Doth it come often in your heart when you are about holy religious exercises? It is an ill token.

Look if the world takes the pre-eminence of God more avowedly, hasting all His matters that it may take up the whole man, but never hasting itself to give God His due; wearying of God, but never of itself. And look if, for a business of the world, your heart will curse God and blaspheme and sin against Him. This is a woeful token.

Look if the world claims the prerogative of quickening your soul: then it is your God. Hath it power to enliven you when most dumpish and indisposed for anything? But the remembrance of all that God hath said or promised in spiritual things doth not so, and hath no power nor influence upon your spirit, to quicken or cherish or raise it up. That is a bad token. Yea, you who are godly, in as far as you feel yourselves guilty in these things, know that you are too far engaged.

From a sermon on Ps. 4:6, 7, *preached* Dec. 27, 1655.

'WHICH A MAN FOUND AND HID'

There is prejudice by venting religion too soon. Profession gets the foregate of both knowledge, faith, and tenderness; and ordinarily there is an ill-holden house afterwards. I may say, through the untimely din of some folks' religion, both godly folk and piety do suffer. It often holds true, they that show their gear long to be robbed. This reproves many who, if they but find some warming in the outer court of affection, proclaim that they have found Christ. Stay a while, till you look about you; the trial follows. But you question me: What shall we do, if we may not vent what we find? Go and examine thy way, by what thou findest in others and their finding of the jewel. Go, look what ado you have had for it, and search your former ways. Bethink what it may cost you, and what you must quit for it. By all means insure it, and hide it till you do insure it.

From a sermon on Matt. 13:44, *preached* July 26, 1656.

HE ABIDETH FAITHFUL

Why is He called the Bridegroom, since the marriage is past between Him and many? There are various answers. Because of the vigour and greenness of love that is still on Him; He 'remembers the love of espousals and kindness of youth'. Because He is still wooing others, and carrying on marriage daily. Because there be some things to perfect to them all, whom He hath married.

What, then, is wanting in that marriage-business, for which Christ must come back to perfect it? There wants full possession of Himself, which we could not bear hereaway; we shall drink of that wine 'new in his kingdom.' We want that equipage that beseems the Lamb's wife; she will be made suitable to Him, when she shall be 'made like his glorious body.' She wants possession of the dowry, of which she hath got but poor investiture hitherto—these rivers of pleasure, these mansions. The saints want a full sight of the Father and of the Son and of the Holy Ghost, whom they shall see no more 'through a glass'. In a word, He is yet to put them in a state, where they shall be not only in a capacity not to fall out of His love, but also out of a capacity of offending Him and of all mistakes of Him.

And these are great things.

From a sermon on Matt. 25:6, *preached* Aug. 18, 1656.

OF HIM, THROUGH HIM, TO HIM

The first failing in our duty is in this, we forget that God is the Lord; especially in one of these three respects:

That of Him are all things. It is He that must prescribe laws, and He that must give knowledge of and respect unto these laws. And He it is whose breath and influence alone make dead dry bones live and move. O, what holy, awful dependency would be on Him in all things, natural and spiritual, if this were believed! But the faith of it must be from Him also.

That through Him are all things. When He hath set them on foot, they cannot continue in their being but through Him, and as they are and have sparkles of His image, and are fluttered over by that Spirit that moved on the waters. O, what self-denial, and adhering to Him, would be here in things which are, as well as in things which are not; for what is, it is as in Him, whence, if it depart, it is nothing, if not worse.

That to Him are all things. Not only is He the last end for whom all things are made, and towards whom they do drive; but the proper end of each being is that God may be made manifest. He will, by all things that are, whatsoever they be, some one way or other appear to be what He is; so that whatsoever is must be to His account and behoof. O, what abstractedness from your created ends and designs, and what reverent submission to His will, would be in men, if folk did practically believe this!

Study to know Him, in these three respects, to be the Lord. It shall contribute much for your duty.

From a sermon on Ps. 45:11, *preached* Aug. 17, 1657.

THE THREE ESSENTIAL TRUTHS

We are become so tasty and dainty in our spiritual food that we can be pleased with nothing which is not curious, singular, and new. But it was never well with us, since we left off to be exercised with the first good substantials of religion. There be three great things which were wont to work kindly with men's hearts: their many transgressions by which they lay open to the wrath of God, the way to be cleared of these things and rescued from the wrath, and how to apply that relief to myself – ugly sin, Christ only precious, and useful faith to grip Him.

From a sermon on Acts 13:39, *preached* June 18, 1659.

PEOPLE ARE SLOW TO BELIEVE

Want of seriousness about the thing on which faith is to be exercised makes men slow to come to believing. When men are not in earnest about their salvation and the matters of Christ's kingdom, they move little towards a heart-grounded persuasion about these things. They are indifferent to them.

There is a weight which 'easily besetteth' men, and this makes them slow towards fixed believing. They are not dead to all things beside. Some are not emptied of their own righteousness, and so do not easily submit to Christ's. And a man being engaged with a present world, whether with his relations or his means, he is slow to close cordially with the kingdom of Christ.

Contrary tides make a slow motion here. If things would keep still in a calm and in a smiling strain, men would move quickly in believing. The disciples moved fast in a fair day, when Christ carried all before Him; but, when the storm was in His face, they halted much.

An ill-shapen bottom causeth a slow motion in a vessel. Whilst men move upon carnal principles of natural reason, the motion towards believing must be slow; they would have reason satisfied in everything. But, if they would bottom themselves on Christ, and move upon principles of the divine nature, leaving things to His wisdom and power to make them out, they were then on a bottom suitable to the designed motion and attainment, and so would move more quickly.

There is some other mistake that occasioneth this slow motion, as that the thing may admit a delay, or that afterwards it may have a more fit season, or that the company is few.

From a sermon on John 16:31, *preached* August 1660.

You say, you dare not venture on Christ. How can you contradict Him who willeth all to venture, who see need, and hath said, there is life in the Son for all who desire it? Will you make head against God's design effectually carried on above five thousand years, and decry the perfect ransom of Christ? Will you offend the whole godly, by alleging the insufficiency of His sacrifice? Well, know that in nothing else you can please God; for 'without faith it is impossible to please him.'

It were fitter you should adventure on Christ, over a thousand things which you cannot answer. Shall it be said in other parts, to His dishonour, that there is one found here who hath a condition that dare not so venture on Him, notwithstanding of all that hath been said of the well-ordered covenant? Will you comply with Satan in such a design to decry Christ? Are you worse than Manasseh, Solomon, Paul, Peter? Do you know a way beyond God, who hath said that in no ways He will cast out? Do you know a stop beyond His utmost, who is able to save to the utmost? Take heed of 'running on the bosses of his buckler.'

Or will any say, you cannot close with Christ? What is this you cannot do? Can you not hunger for Him, nor look to Him, nor be pleased with that salvation, nor open your mouth that He may fill it? Do not difficult the way to heaven, for that derogates much from all He hath done.

From a sermon on Luke 22:31, *preached* July 14, 1662.

HEAVEN'S EASY, ARTLESS, UNENCUMBERED PLAN

The way of salvation is now most easy. *It is nigh thee*, that is, the matter is not far off, either in heaven or in hell; it is at man s hand and may be quickly reaclied. *It is in thy mouth*; poor men may now express and speak the business, and every man hath it in his mouth – it is so notour (*ie.*, notorious) and known. *It is in thine heart*, that is, the thoughts of man can fathom it, it is so plain; it is no mysterious thing; neither is it a business of great outward oration or observation, it is a thing transacted in the heart and inward affection; if the heart be to it, it is won. It is a thing which is *preached* by poor simple men, and is secretly conveyed into men by preaching the Gospel; so that we are not to expect any extraordinary revelation or communication about this matter, but even to close with it in the offer of the Word. In a word, it is *of faith*.

Well then, since all is resolved into faith, we must show that faith is in some respect an easy thing.

Is not that easy which, if a man seriously desire it, he hath it? Such a thing salvation now is, and its condition; 'blessed are they that hunger, for they shall be filled.' Is not that easy, whereunto if a man move, he hath it? Such a thing is this; if he but 'flee for refuge to take hold on the hope set before him', it is his. Is not that easy after which if a man greedily look with his heart, he hath it? Such a thing is this; if he but look to Him, he is saved. Is not that easy, which a man gets by loving the market where it is, although he have nothing to buy it with? Such a thing is this; 'come without money', says Isaiah. Is not that an easy thing, which a man hath if he will but take it when it is offered to him? Such a thing is this; if you *receive*, all is your own. Is it not an easy thing, which a man hath, if he will but let Another fasten it on him, if he will but open his mouth and let God put it in – open his hand and let God lay it in his loof (*i.e.*, the palm of the hand)? Such a thing is this. In a word, is it not an easy thing, which a man hath as soon as he begins to think highly of it, and to value it? So Christ is precious to those who believe.

O, how easy a business is salvation now made for poor weak man! May we not say that, the matter being of faith, it is properly of grace; and so the promise is sure to all the seed, weak and strong?

From a sermon on Rom. 10:6–9, *preached in* 1662.

THE BRIDE COMES TO THE WEDDING FEAST

In approaching to the Table of the Lord, remember it is very unbeseeming that, in the day and hour of espousals, the bride should be dirty, and have known spots on her, which she assayeth not to put off. It is true, at first Christ taketh a dirty bride by the hand, and hath her often to wash afterwards. But now, in this solemn confirmation of marriage, a filthy bride, with known iniquity cleaving to her with her own consent, is a dreadful thing.

A drowsy bride is shameful, when so solemn a transaction is in doing before so many witnesses. Then to be sleepy and drowsy doth portend somewhat. It is true, the three disciples did sleep, and were very heavy, quickly after, in a great choke (*i.e.*, stress or crisis). But that was the forerunner of a sad defection.

A diverted bride is unseemly. To be under diversion and distraction in such a solemnity as this speaks rank corruption, and little of the awe and fear of God, and small esteem of Christ Jesus. How unbeseeming were it for a bride in presence of the bridegroom, when before witnesses she is to give her marriage consent, or to ratify it, even then to be dallying with other things, although they should be the gifts received from the bridegroom!

A diffident bride is very unseemly. In the very hour when the Bridegroom hath called all His friends together, to be witnesses of what He hath done and said for her satisfaction, and whilst He is communicating to her the highest and clearest and surest pledge of love He can, putting His great seal to all the charters of the Covenant, after they are read over and over – yet to look down, and to be jealous, and to say in your heart, 'He is but mocking me,' it is a great provocation. Be not therefore unbelieving but believing.

Before the Observance of the Lord's Supper, in Fenwick Church, 1662.